SINGAPORE 2(

THE CITY AT A GLANCE

GN00836485

Marina Bay Financial Centre
This Kohn Pedersen Fox-designed mega
complex – comprising office towers, sh(
and apartment blocks – is the centrepie(
of a second, still-evolving business distri(...
Marina Boulevard

The Sail @ Marina Bay
Designed by Timothy Johnson and Peter Pran
of NBBJ, the city's tallest condominium tower
was inspired by a sail catching the wind.
Marina Boulevard

Clifford Pier
Once, immigrants landed here, but these days
this 1933 building houses The Fullerton Bay
Hotel's lobby and a smart Chinese restaurant.
80 Collyer Quay

The Fullerton Hotel
Opened in 1928, the former post and tax office
was restored to its full Palladian glory in 2000.
The outdoor pool has spectacular views.
1 Fullerton Square, T 6733 8388

OCBC Centre
A reminder of the city's brief flirtation with
brutalism, IM Pei's 1976 concrete slab was
once the tallest building in South-East Asia.
65 Chulia Street

Victoria Concert Hall
The 1905 neoclassical erstwhile town hall,
set to reopen in 2015 after renovations, is
home to the Singapore Symphony Orchestra.
11 Empress Place, T 6338 1230

Esplanade
DP Architects and Michael Wilford & Partners'
performing arts centre opened in 2002, and
is distinguished by its aluminium-clad domes.
1 Esplanade Drive, T 6828 8377

INTRODUCTION
THE CHANGING FACE OF THE URBAN SCENE

Time was when Singapore had a deserved reputation for being a soulless, air-conditioned metropolis. Its claims to fame were the shop-fest of Orchard Road and a list of banned activities, including littering and selling *Cosmopolitan*. The new Singapore still has the retail obsession and state control, but over a decade or so it has transformed its social and cultural scenes into a vibrant crucible of cuisine, art, fashion and sport, taking neighbours like Australia, Thailand and Japan by surprise. These are the best of times. The F1 Grand Prix is a fixture, the city hosts the World Architecture Festival, and the concert halls are now a must for touring rock acts.

For a snapshot of Singapore's ambitions, look to the massive development on Marina Bay, where a glitzy casino resort appeared out of nowhere and a new CBD is in the making. The burgeoning restaurant scene, crowded with cash-rich locals and expats fleeing Europe's woes, is a stunning sweep of local flavours and Pan-Asian techniques. The confidence that you feel on the streets is authentic, whether in the lively rooftop bars that seem to spring up every day, in art hubs housed in refurbished army barracks, or in the bold new architecture by the likes of Zarch Collaboratives and WOHA.

Head out to Sentosa Island. Yes, the beach is manmade and the main attractions are Universal Studios and Resorts World Sentosa, but in the shrieks of excitement you can hear the future of this city-state: the sound of a buttoned-up people finally having fun.

ESSENTIAL INFO

FACTS, FIGURES AND USEFUL ADDRESSES

TOURIST OFFICE
Singapore Visitors Centre
Orchard Road/Cairnhill Road
T 1800 736 2000
www.yoursingapore.com

TRANSPORT
Airport transfer to city centre
Shuttle buses to several hotels can be
booked at the airport. The fare is S$9
www.changiairport.com
Car hire
Avis
T 6737 1688
Metro
Trains run from roughly 6am to 12am
www.smrt.com.sg
Taxis
CityCab
T 6552 1111
Travel card
A three-day Tourist Pass costs S$20

EMERGENCY SERVICES
Ambulance/Fire
T 995
Police
T 999
Late-night pharmacy (until 12am)
Silver Cross Medical Centre
275a Holland Avenue
T 6462 2818

EMBASSIES AND CONSULATES
British High Commission
100 Tanglin Road
T 6424 4200
www.gov.uk/government/world/singapore
US Embassy
27 Napier Road
T 6476 9100
singapore.usembassy.gov

POSTAL SERVICES
Post office
2-2 Hitachi Tower
16 Collyer Quay
Shipping
FedEx
T 1800 743 2626
www.fedex.com/sg

BOOKS
**A Guide to 21st Century Singapore
Architecture** by Patrick Bingham-Hall
(Pesaro)
Can Asians Think? by Kishore
Mahbubani (Marshall Cavendish Intl Asia)
Singapore Shophouse by Julian Davison
and Luca Invernizzi Tettoni (Laurence King)

WEBSITES
Art
www.acm.org.sg
Newspapers
www.businesstimes.com.sg
www.straitstimes.com

EVENTS
Singapore Biennale
www.singaporebiennale.org
World Architecture Festival
www.worldarchitecturefestival.com

COST OF LIVING
Taxi from Changi Airport to city centre
S$35
Cappuccino
S$4.70
Packet of cigarettes
S$11
Daily newspaper
S$0.90
Bottle of champagne
S$80

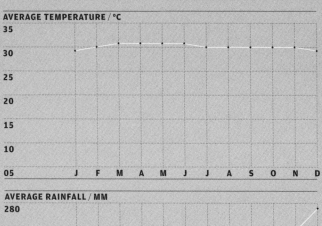

SINGAPORE
Population
5.4 million
Currency
Singapore dollar
Telephone code
Singapore: 65
Local time
GMT +8
Flight time
London: 13 hours

Delhi
Guangzhou   Hong Kong
Hanoi
Mumbai
Manila
Bangkok
Ho Chi Minh City
MALAYSIA
□ **Singapore**

AVERAGE TEMPERATURE / °C

		J	F	M	A	M	J	J	A	S	O	N	D
35													
30													
25													
20													
15													
10													
05													

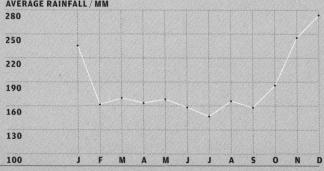

AVERAGE RAINFALL / MM

		J	F	M	A	M	J	J	A	S	O	N	D
280													
250													
220													
190													
160													
130													
100													

NEIGHBOURHOODS

THE AREAS YOU NEED TO KNOW AND WHY

To help you navigate the city, we've chosen the most interesting districts (see below and the map inside the back cover) and colour-coded our featured venues, according to their location; those venues that are outside these areas are not coloured.

ORCHARD ROAD

Singapore's mini-answer to New York's Fifth Avenue, Orchard Road is bookended by the Orchard Parade Hotel (1 Tanglin Road, T 6737 1133) and Plaza Singapura. In-between is a shopaholic's dream of high-end boutiques and marbled emporiums, as well as many of the top hotels. The vast ION Orchard (see p010), Paragon and Ngee Ann City malls are stomping grounds for the Prada set, and Christina Ong's trendy Club 21 is next to the Four Seasons (see p028).

TANJONG PAGAR

Few areas of Singapore can evoke as great a feeling of place and identity as Tanjong Pagar. Just south of the Singapore River, it boasts quaint reminders of the city's past. Elaborate Indian and Chinese temples and bustling markets jostle with bijoux stores and outré bars/nightspots such as Taboo (65-67 Neil Road) and Does Your Mother Know (41 Neil Road, T 6224 3965).

RAFFLES PLACE

Taking its name from the country's colonial founder, Sir Stamford Raffles, the Central Business District, assembled around the mouth of the Singapore River, composes an extraordinary skyline. Some of the city's tallest skyscrapers, such as Kenzo Tange's UOB Plaza One (80 Raffles Place), rear up over Boat Quay's neat rows of old shophouses. Many of these have been converted into noisy (and rather touristy) discos, pubs, cafés and restaurants.

LITTLE INDIA

Atmospheric and cacophonous, Little India's labyrinth of roads and alleys are dense with the smells and noise of mother India, although it is considerably more sanitised. The streets are rammed with a bewildering array of silks, gold, spices, silverware and wood carvings, as well as boutique hotels such as Moon (see p026) and Loh Lik Peng's inventive Wanderlust (see p016). The South Indian restaurants here pack in the curry-hungry crowds.

BALESTIER

North of Orchard Road, Balestier was once a bucolic retreat for the city's well-to-do. Today, it is a quarter full of historical and architectural landmarks. The main stretch, Balestier Road, wraps around the base of a low hill, taking in many of Singapore's finest colonial houses and the 1847 Goh Chor Tua Pek Kong temple (No 249), which has a freestanding Chinese opera stage.

KATONG

This district remains one of Singapore's better-kept secrets. Whereas the rest of the island continues to obsess over shiny skyscrapers, Katong, nestled in the eastern suburbs, remains stubbornly anchored to a gentler past. The landscape comprises sedately ageing shophouses and bungalows, which host numerous excellent dining spots — try the Nyonya dumplings at Kim Choo Kueh Chang Babi (60-62 Joo Chiat Place, T 6344 0830).

LANDMARKS

THE SHAPE OF THE CITY SKYLINE

Singapore is a small country: it takes barely an hour to zip from one end of the diamond-shaped island to the other. There is no real capital city as such – the administrative headquarters, the parliament building included, are scattered across the island. That said, most of the attractions and hotels are clustered in the south, around Orchard Road in particular. A long-established shopping and entertainment hub, it continues to grow – witness the phallic tribute to consumerism that is ION (overleaf). Further south is the CBD, bounded by Raffles Place, Tanjong Pagar and Marina Bay. It is here that Singapore's skyline is changing, notably with the opening of Moshe Safdie's 200m-high Marina Bay Sands (see p078) in 2011, a resort which has three towers housing a hotel, a casino, a luxury mall, a convention centre, a museum and myriad restaurants.

Some 10 minutes away is a necklace of rainforest and aerial walkways that begins at Mount Faber Park and winds through to Telok Blangah Hill Park (see p089). Out to the west are industrial estates and suburbs piled high with public housing; in the south are green pockets like the Spice Garden at Fort Canning Park (River Valley Road). The north is sprinkled with reservoirs and is home to the Night Safari (80 Mandai Lake Road, T 6269 3411), and the east, dominated by Changi Airport, is an enclave of the Peranakans, descendants of Chinese immigrants and indigenous Malays.
For full addresses, see Resources.

ION Orchard

Opened in 2009, ION has quickly become a landmark on Orchard Road. Its 218m steel-and-glass frame is supposed to resemble an upside-down tropical flower, although locals have suggested a less savoury comparison. Designed by London-based architects Benoy, the structure's 'petals' – sheathed by a curtain of coloured lights – house 64,000 sq m of bold-faced boutiques, such as Louis Vuitton, Prada, Cartier and Dior, over eight levels, four of which are underground. The 'stem' (56 storeys of private apartments) towers over the strip. Within the complex there is also 500 sq m of gallery space, used to exhibit contemporary and multimedia art. Tunnels connect to the Ngee Ann City shopping mall (T 6827 9512) and its Takashimaya department store (T 6738 1111), a boon on monsoon-washed days. *2 Orchard Turn, T 6238 8228, www.ionorchard.com*

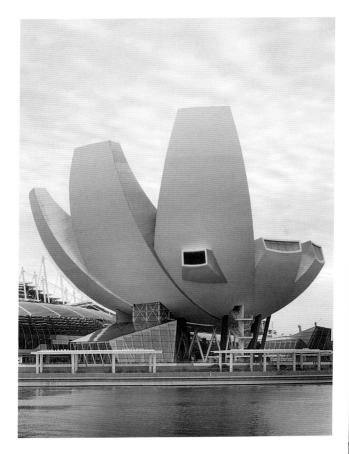

ArtScience Museum

Even seen from a distance, Moshe Safdie's all-white design, right on the Marina Bay water, is an eye-catching beauty. Its form is derived from intersecting, overlapping spheroids which, depending on who you talk to, takes the form of a giant lotus or a ten-fingered human-shaped hand. Inside, the white curvilinear space wraps around a central oculus and waterfall that feeds an interior pond, filling the gallery spaces with natural light. The informative Asian-themed exhibits, which have included retrospectives on Genghis Khan and Silk Road treasures, are particularly well done, revealing just enough factoids to avoid museum fatigue. When you've finished, hit the luxury mega-mall in the nearby Marina Bay Sands resort (see p078). *10 Bayfront Avenue, T 6688 8868, www.marinabaysands.com*

Suntec City

This multipurpose complex – location of the Singapore International Convention & Exhibition Centre – consists of four 45-storey towers and an 18-storey block linked around an enormous brazier-like fountain. Owned by Hong Kong property tycoon Li Ka-shing, Suntec City, opened in 1998, was designed by architects Tsao & McKown. Rumour has it that the brief was to position the towers in such a way that from the air they resemble a cupped hand (the shorter tower being the thumb). The hand supposedly represents Li Ka-shing's as he holds the fortunes, refilled by the fountain, of his tenants. In a country where feng shui is an obsession, and doors are regularly tilted at an angle for a smoother flow of luck, hardly anyone blinks an eye.

3 Temasek Boulevard,
www.sunteccity.com.sg

Pearl Bank

Towering above a flat neighbourhood of shophouses and low-rise office blocks, Pearl Bank has been a local landmark since it was unveiled by architect Tan Cheng Siong in 1976. It was an innovative structure in a number of ways, not least for its unusual hollow circular shape. At 38 storeys, it was also the tallest residential building in Asia at the time. To spread the load, Tan Cheng Siong set Pearl Bank's 272 apartments around 10 radial walls that rise through its entire height. Along with the structural columns and lift cores, this configuration facilitates the intricate massing of the living spaces. A threatened sale (and probable demolition) in 2008 was narrowly averted after a concerted campaign by outraged residents and architectural conservationists.

1 Pearl Bank

HOTELS
WHERE TO STAY AND WHICH ROOMS TO BOOK

For years, Singaporean hotels have defaulted to a safe but bland marble-and-chintz look. However, the service is usually superior to their European equivalents, thus attracting Indonesian, Hong Kong and Taiwanese tycoons and their Gucci-adorned wives. Most larger chains are along Orchard Road, including the St Regis (29 Tanglin Road, T 6506 6888) and Regent (see p022), whereas the Shangri-La (22 Orange Grove Road, T 6737 3644) and a clutch of four-stars hold court on the arterial roads. Closer to the water are big-hitters such as Raffles (1 Beach Road, T 6337 1886), Marina Bay Sands (10 Bayfront Avenue, T 6688 8868) and The Fullerton Bay Hotel (80 Collyer Quay, T 6333 8388), not forgetting the newly opened Westin (12 Marina View, Asia Square Tower, T 6922 6888).

More recently, savvy hoteliers have launched hip properties in up-and-coming districts such as Chinatown and Tanjong Pagar. Elsewhere, boutiques include Hotel Fort Canning (11 Canning Walk, T 6559 6769), The Club (28 Ann Siang Road, T 6808 2188), set in a row of converted shophouses, and Wangz Hotel (231 Outram Road, T 6595 1388), where the rooftop bar has fabulous sunset views. Loh Lik Peng brings the fun with Wanderlust (2 Dickson Road, T 6396 3322), while newbies include the W (21 Ocean Way, T 6808 7288), TreeTop Lofts (Resorts World Sentosa, 8 Sentosa Gateway, T 6577 8899) and Sofitel So (35 Robinson Road).
For full addresses and room rates, see Resources.

Capella

In 2009, Foster + Partners, in collaboration with DP Architects, transformed an 1880s British military mess hall sited on Sentosa Island into a resort that is only missing a beach. This hasn't stopped the jeunesse dorée from flocking to Capella's spa and open-air Bob's Bar, which overlooks the three cascading pools (above). New wings with huge steel shades are hidden behind the original red-roofed mansion, and two officers' bungalows were converted into luxury three-bedroom Colonial Manors. Interior designer Jaya Ibrahim gave the 112 accommodations a low-key dose of Bali chic, using granite or marble in the bathrooms. All villas and manors have plunge pools or jacuzzis, and Premier Seaview Room 410 has great ocean vistas. *1 The Knolls, Sentosa Island, T 6377 8888, www.capellasingapore.com*

Parkroyal on Pickering
Opened in 2013, Singapore's first green
hotel employs a host of eco initiatives
that fully exploit the city's abundance
of sunshine and rain. Local architects
WOHA have designed a light-filled space,
furnished in soothing green and woodsy
hues (Orchid Club Lounge, pictured). The
367-room oasis also has a wellness floor
with an infinity pool overlooking the CBD.
3 Upper Pickering Street, T 6809 8888

The Ritz-Carlton Millenia

Framed by lush foliage and Marina Bay, The Ritz-Carlton is a byword for lap-it-up luxury. Designed by Pritzker Prize-winning architect Kevin Roche of KRJDA (public spaces are by Howard Hirsch), the hotel is approached via a sinuous, green-canopied driveway. Guests step out into a 12m-high lobby of Italian marble, crowned by Frank Stella's spectacular *Cornucopia* (opposite). The corridors are like mini-museums, displaying more than 4,200 paintings and art installations, including pieces by David Hockney, Andy Warhol and Henry Moore. This hasn't come at the cost of comfort, however. Every room was made-over by Burega Farnell in 2011, using a soft palette of pale timber, creamy faux leather wall panelling and white marble floor tiles. We recommend Premier Suite 3126 (above), which has views over the Singapore Flyer. *7 Raffles Avenue, T 6337 8888, www.ritzcarlton.com*

Regent

More than three decades old, the Regent continues to pull in a discerning business crowd who are drawn to its understated but sunny mix of service, locally rated restaurants and architect John Portman's soaring ziggurat atrium housing Michio Ihara's shimmering *Singapore Shower* sculpture (left). The rooms are dressed in neutral tones with an East meets West blend of chinoiserie furniture, South-East Asian art, mustard-gold upholstery and L'Occitane products. Check into Room 1133 for its satisfying views across the treetops along Orchard Boulevard. Dining options include the tempura at Tenshin (T 6735 4588), delicate dim sum at the renovated Summer Palace (T 6725 3288), and Italian classics and tasty handcrafted desserts at Basilico (T 6725 3232), where patrons also enjoy the benefits of a walk-in wine cellar.
*1 Cuscaden Road, T 6733 8888,
www.regenthotels.com/singapore*

New Majestic Hotel

The Majestic arrived here in 2006, riding the wave of 'New Asia' art and design. The colonial-era building was stripped out and redesigned by DP Architects and interior designer Colin Seah, who put together a pleasingly sparse space, notably the lobby, which boasts an exposed concrete ceiling. Clever touches include the rooftop pool (above), that has portholes in the bottom through which you can peer into the fine

Majestic Restaurant (T 6511 4718). The 30 rooms have been decorated by nine local creatives, among them fashion designer Wykidd Song and the Wallpaper* Design Award-recipient Patrick Chia. Reserve a spacious Attic Suite for its twin antique bathtubs, or perhaps a Premier Garden Room (opposite) for the hanging bed.
31-37 Bukit Pasoh Road, T 6511 4700, www.newmajestichotel.com

Moon
First-time hotelier Billy Ong may have
set Moon amid the chaos of Little India,
but the property's warm, muted decor
works in direct contrast. The interiors
and architecture are by local outfit
Formwerkz, and this bolthole also
benefits from great hawker food stalls
and two MRT train stations nearby.
Reserve the Moonlight Suite (pictured).
23 Dickson Road, T 6827 6666

Four Seasons
One of Singapore's grandes dames since 1994, the Four Seasons is noted as much for its first-rate service as for its top-flight Club 21 shopping arcade boasting labels such as The Row, Dries Van Noten and Carven. Created by Singapore Architects Association and interior designers Hirsch Bedner Associates, the hotel's generously proportioned rooms feature floral motifs, absurdly soft beds and elegantly marbled bathrooms. Check into an Executive Suite (left) or Room 1603, which has one of the property's best panoramas, over the ION complex (see p010). The Jiang-Nan Chun (T 6831 7220) Cantonese restaurant is still a draw for bigwigs and gourmands, and bistro-grill One-Ninety (T 6831 7250) serves excellent seafood and meat dishes.
190 Orchard Boulevard, T 6734 1110, www.fourseasons.com/singapore

Naumi Liora

The Hind Group's second Singapore hotel
taps into Keong Saik Road's colourful buzz
of upmarket restaurants – including Brit
chef Jason Atherton's tapas joint, Esquina
(T 6222 1616) – local *tze-char* (homestyle)
hawker stalls and bars. Designer Gaurang
Khemka has kept the bones of the colonial-
styled shophouse in Chinatown fully intact,
including the original timber flooring and
windows; and the interiors are furnished
with a blend of modern and Peranakan
flourishes, such as Nespresso machines
and chinoiserie woodwork. The 24-hour
complimentary snack bar in the lobby
(above), stocked with ice-cream, teas and
pastries, is a nice touch. Of the 79 rooms,
the best face Keong Saik Road, although
for pure tropical escapism book the Liora
Porch (opposite), complete with garden
patio that overlooks Duxton Plain Park.
55 Keong Saik Road, T 6922 9000,
www.naumiliora.com

24 HOURS

SEE THE BEST OF THE CITY IN JUST ONE DAY

It used to be that 24 hours in Singapore was enough. Not now. You may have to crisscross the island a few times to get the most out of it, but you'll rarely journey longer than 30 minutes. Taxis can be hard to find during rush hour, but the MRT is fast and efficient, and its network is growing. Make time for modern Asian art at Gajah Gallery (1-8 MICA Building, 140 Hill Street, T 6737 4202), before dropping into contemporary design museum Red Dot (28 Maxwell Road, T 6327 8027). The government's push to turn Singapore into a regional art centre continues apace: leading that drive is the construction of the country's first National Art Gallery in the old Supreme Court and City Hall, a vast project by Studio Milou that will link the two buildings via a glass canopy on opening in 2015.

It's easy to eat well here. If you're on a flying visit, breakfast on soft boiled eggs and toast spread with *kaya* (coconut and pandan leaf jam) at Chin Mee Chin (204 East Coast Road, T 6345 0419), or dim sum at Swee Choon (183 Jalan Besar, T 6225 7788) or the local outpost of Hong Kong's Tim Ho Wan (1-29a Plaza Singapura, 68 Orchard Road, T 6251 2000), followed by an informative trip to the Chinatown Heritage Centre (48 Pagoda Street, T 6221 9556). Dine out in style at The White Rabbit (39c Harding Road, T 6473 9965), before ending the day with some hot caramel doughnuts at Keong Saik Snacks (49 Keong Saik Road, T 6221 8338). *For full addresses, see Resources.*

10.00 The Intan

To step into collector Alvin Yapp's home, set in a row of beautifully preserved early 20th-century terraced houses, is to travel deep into the heart of Peranakan culture. A private museum since 2011, The Intan holds an amazing collection of artefacts sourced from Penang, Malacca, England, China and India. These cover every single surface, although the space never strays into kitsch or clutter. Almost all aspects of Peranakan life are represented, from local teak furniture, carved ancestral altars and ceremonial costumes to rare porcelain bowls, embroidered *kebayas* (traditional blouses) and beaded slippers. Yapp offers private one-hour tours that culminate in an assortment of traditional snacks. Visits are by appointment only.
69 Joo Chiat Terrace, T 6440 1148, www.the-intan.com

12.00 Gillman Barracks

It cost S$10m to transform a former 1930s barracks into Singapore's new arts centre. The complex houses a series of exhibition spaces and palm-fringed cafés, as well as the CCA (Centre for Contemporary Art), where artists, curators and collectors are invited to congregate, lecture and work in residence. The 17 galleries include major Asian players such as ShanghART, Kyoto's Tomio Koyama and Tokyo's Kaikai Kiki, while Future Perfect stages intriguing shows from artists like Charles Lim ('Sea State 3: Inversion', above), thanks to the broad experience of curators such as Nina Miall, once a director of London's Haunch of Venison. Set amid a literal jungle rather than a concrete one, Gillman Barracks offers the antithesis of the modern Asian gallery experience. Closed Mondays.
9 Lock Road, www.gillmanbarracks.com

14.00 Open Door Policy

In a city whose ethnic quarters can seem a little like Disney theme parks, there's a genuine vibe to the Tiong Bahru district. Among a charming mix of hawker stalls, Buddhist temples and early 1950s art deco-style flats, is the Spa Esprit Group's venture, Open Door Policy, or ODP as locals call it. Creative director Jerry De Souza has made the most of the deep, narrow space in this prewar shophouse, bouncing light off the embossed, tin-lined ceiling and installing a glass-encased kitchen along one of the walls. The menu is an eclectic mix of contemporary French bistro and comfort fare, and there's an unusually sophisticated coffee selection courtesy of 40 Hands (T 6225 8545), based across the road. Closed Tuesdays.
19 Yong Siak Street, T 6221 9307, www.odpsingapore.com

The Fall

16.00 Gardens by the Bay

The 101-hectare Gardens by the Bay, designed by UK-based Grant Associates and Wilkinson Eyre, is the latest salvo in Singapore's utopian rebranding as a tropical garden city where lush greenery enfolds 21st-century skyscrapers. Opened in 2012, the crown jewel of the three vast waterfront gardens is a 54-hectare twin-conservatory complex, dubbed Bay South Garden. Sheathed in steel and glass, the asymmetrical, ribbed biodomes are futuristic in their silhouette, their raison d'être telegraphed by glimpses of the plant life within, comprising more than 1,600 species from across the planet. The cool and misty Cloud Forest (above) houses high-altitude tropical plants clinging to the sides of a 35m-tall faux mountain.
18 Marina Gardens Drive, T 6420 6848, www.gardensbythebay.com.sg

18.30 Ku Dé Ta

At any time of the day or night, the view at Ku Dé Ta dazzles with its wraparound sweep of Singapore's skyline. Making the most of its literally high-profile address, the restaurant/bar/club crowns Marina Bay Sands' 200m-high SkyPark. It's a magnet for pretty young things and big shots in search of a meal or a cocktail before they head down to the casino.

1 Bayfront Avenue, T 6688 7688

URBAN LIFE
CAFÉS, RESTAURANTS, BARS AND NIGHTCLUBS

Despite what Malaysians from across the Johor Straits might say, Singapore is a food mecca. The diaspora of youthful talent who returned from London, New York, Paris and Sydney in the late 20th-century brought new culinary concepts; their menus now stretch from Sardinian dishes at Sopra (1-2, 10 Claymore Road, T 6737 3253) and Peranakan fusion at Violet Oon's Kitchen (881 Bukit Timah Road, T 6468 5430) to pork belly tacos at Lower East Side Taqueria (19 East Coast Road, T 6348 1302) and the modern Asian bar snacks at Ding Dong (23 Ann Siang Road, T 6557 0189).

Street fare is unbeatable, and is available for a song in bustling coffee shops and open-air hawker centres in the suburbs. Entire quarters have their own specialities – sample Peranakan classics in Katong, pepper crab on the East Coast and fish-head curries in Little India. Pick up the local Makansutra guide to hawker fare (www.makansutra.com) or visit the raucous Chomp Chomp Food Centre in Serangoon Gardens (20 Kensington Park Road).

Meanwhile, the city's party scene belies its prissy reputation abroad. Zouk (see p056) serves up a heady combo of electro and trance; Level 33 (Tower 1, Marina Bay Financial Centre, 8 Marina Boulevard, T 6834 3133) boasts skyline views; and the speakeasy Jekyll & Hyde (49 Tras Street, T 6222 3349) makes its mark with a menu of manicures to go with rounds of killer cocktails.
For full addresses, see Resources.

Forest

After a decade as culinary director at the TungLok Group, Sam Leong branched out on his own in 2012 with the launch of Forest. Set in a hotel resort on Sentosa Island, the restaurant showcases Leong's deft touch and affinity for contemporary Chinese cuisine. Australian Diana Simpson designed the rainforest-inspired interior: a bright, high-ceilinged dining room where an open kitchen is segmented by stylised faux trees. Leong's innovative menu includes milky chicken broth with morel mushrooms and wild bamboo pith, and pan-seared foie gras with smoked duck breast on homemade crispy bean curd. There are also dishes that display Thai touches, such as steamed cod fillet with ginger flower, lemon and Kaffir lime leaves.

Level One, Equarius Hotel, 8 Sentosa Gateway, T 6577 7788, www.rwsentosa.com

Saint Pierre

After closing his much loved Saint Pierre
in the CBD, chef/owner Emmanuel
Stroobant has pitched up in the more
bucolic Sentosa Cove marina. The new
space, by local design firm Terre, serves
a lush mod-European surf-and-turf menu
that has long-time fans raving about
the roasted lobster with braised fennel,
grilled courgette, tomatoes and basil.
1-15 Quayside Isle, 31 Ocean Way

Oxwell & Co

Ann Siang Road is experiencing something of a renaissance, its rows of restored fin de siècle shophouses now bristling with upmarket boutiques and restaurants, like Oxwell & Co. This high-ceilinged space is furnished with industrial flair by way of recycled furniture and vintage lights, but it's the artisanal beers and cocktails, siphoned through wooden kegs and a maze of exposed copper piping, that have made it such a success. Head bartender Luke Whearty makes standards with gusto and respect: the house gin and tonic is infused with fresh local nutmeg and homemade clove tonic water. Mark Sargeant heads up the dining room (above), sending out modern British dishes such as pressed ham hock with mustard mayonnaise. *5 Ann Siang Road, T 6438 3984, www.oxwellandco.com*

Pollen

British chef Jason Atherton's love affair with Singapore continues. Following his lauded 2011 pintxos restaurant Esquina (see p030), he teamed up with hotelier Loh Lik Peng to open Pollen at Gardens by the Bay (see p037) the following year. The Colombian architect Antonio Eraso has carved out a light-filled corner of the glass-sheathed Flower Dome and bordered the space with a dense green wall and a working garden that supplies herbs and vegetables for the kitchen. Fans of Atherton will delight in the mod-Euro menu, which includes seasonal delights such as cured foie gras with smoked passion fruit, almonds and muscovado, and Wagyu beef cheek with glazed salsify and mushroom duxelles. *1-9, 18 Marina Gardens Drive, T 6604 9988, www.pollen.com.sg*

Tanjong Beach Club

Opened in 2010, this secluded, sun-kissed throwback to 1950s beachside glamour was styled by nightlife impresarios The Lo & Behold Group. The space gives off a nostalgic vibe, and glass, wood and stone blur the lines between interior and exterior. The chic dining room dishes up tasty grilled meat and seafood, and the centrepiece outdoor bar is accented by hand-painted tiles. A 20m infinity pool, flanked by rows of daybeds, extends on to the beach where a mix of expats and local buff young things take in the sun while brazenly people watching. Drop by on a weekend for a brunch of Maine lobster omelette, a signature Tajong Sling (vodka, elderflower, apple juice, lychee, Kaffir lime leaf and ginger) and a volleyball game.
120 Tanjong Beach Walk, Sentosa Island, T 9750 5323, www.tanjongbeachclub.com

StraitsKitchen

It cost a weighty S$7.5m to produce this slick, market-style restaurant, which was designed by Japanese firm Super Potato. Tucked away on the ground floor of the Grand Hyatt, the dramatic space features the interior design firm's trademark steel trim with timber and marble finishes. The menu runs the gamut of the island's varied cuisines, from Chinese – fried rice, noodles; to Indian – tandoori aloo, prawn masala; and Malay – beef rendang, satay. From behind a glass screen, the kitchen cooks up favourites, including traditional desserts such as *mien jiang kueh* (pancake with grated coconut, red bean paste and peanuts). Some locals grouse at S$8.50 fruit juices and steep prices for simple dishes, but the crowds keep on coming.
Grand Hyatt, 10 Scotts Road, T 7632 1234, www.singapore.grand.hyattrestaurants.com

New Asia
Perched on floors 71 and 72 of Swissôtel
The Stamford (T 6338 8585), New Asia bar
draws a crowd of Singaporean TV celebs,
and boasts dizzying views of the city,
as Malaysia and Indonesia twinkle in the
distance. If you feel the floor is tilting,
don't blame it on your G&T, it slants at a
20-degree angle for a better panorama.
*Swissôtel The Stamford, 2 Stamford Road,
T 9177 7307, www.swissotel.com*

OverEasy

The decor of this stylish bar/restaurant, conceived by designers Takenouchi Webb, pays homage to an American diner. There is red booth seating, a concrete and black-granite-topped bar backed by tinted mirrors, and veneered walnut on the walls and curved ceiling. Outside, the riverside terrace has stunning views of Marina Bay. From Wednesday to Saturday, the space mutates into a fully fledged DJ lounge and cocktail bar – try the espresso martini. A supper menu of American comfort food, such as cheesesteak sliders, haystack fries, milkshakes and blueberry waffles, is served until 2am at the weekends, so you've got no excuse to call it a night. Especially as hipster hangout The Butter Factory (T 6333 8243) is directly upstairs. *1-6 One Fullerton, 1 Fullerton Road, T 6423 0701, www.overeasy.com.sg*

The Providore

Although it's ostensibly a glitzy high-end fashion mall, the Mandarin Gallery is fast turning into a gastronomic destination, containing among its haul an outpost of Japanese ramen hotspot Ippudo (T 6235 2797). A recent addition is The Providore, a venture between Bruce Chapman and Robert Collick, former owners of Jones the Grocer (see p059). The all-day diner was designed by Japanese-based Daiki Ozaki

with a retro-industrial vibe that recalls a 1940s architect studio. After browsing through a wall of gourmet teas and the display of freshly baked goods, settle in for beef ragu on grilled polenta or lobster mac and cheese. Save the Spanish baked eggs, and ricotta pancakes with candied walnuts, for a leisurely weekend brunch.
2-5 Mandarin Gallery, 333a Orchard Road, T 6732 1565, www.theprovidore.com

Horse's Mouth Bar

Finding the Horse's Mouth can be tricky. Either enter through a hidden door that adjoins a basement kaiseki restaurant, or at the bottom of the staircase of a ramen joint. The effort is rewarded by a dark 34-seater izakaya bar area that local designers Asylum fitted with a raised bar, framed by back-lit alcoves decorated with origami sakura flowers. Early-bird diners swear by the tonkotsu ramen and sashimi, but it's the superbly crafted drinks that draw the post-prandial crowd. Although purists will prefer the straight shots of sake and rare Japanese whiskies, the cocktail menu constantly evolves thanks to experimental bartenders. The top hits have included a potent concoction comprising gin, cherry tomatoes, pineapple and lychee liqueur.
B1-39 Forum The Shopping Mall,
583 Orchard Road, T 6235 1088

Zouk

The city's premier nightspot may have launched back in 1991, but Zouk has seen off a slew of copycats and pretenders to the throne. The club's core crowd leans towards young, die-hard party stompers, but there is no faulting the line-up of DJs who play house, electro and techno here. Luminaries such as Avicii, Marco Carola and Dash Berlin have all headlined. *17 Jiak Kim Street, T 6738 2988*

Royal China

It was a daring move by Royal China (an outpost of the London restaurant group founded in 1996) to entrust its renovation to Singapore-based Ministry of Design. Known for its theatricality, the design firm was never going to play it safe, and the classical Chinese interiors were replaced with ash flooring, quilted wall coverings and metal mesh curtains in shades of gold. The startling duck-egg-blue colour scheme was inspired by the cheongsam brocade that lead designer Colin Seah saw when he visited Beijing. On the Cantonese menu, lobster fried noodles and stacked, steaming bamboo baskets of delicately wrought dim sum – on which the group has made its name – are reliably good.
3-9 Raffles Arcade, Raffles Hotel,
328 North Bridge Road, T 6412 1330,
www.royalchinasingapore.com

Jones The Grocer

Although a second outlet of this Australian deli chain opened in the Mandarin Gallery (T 6836 6372) in 2010, and a third (T 6884 5597) at ION Orchard (see p010) in 2013, the original Jones The Grocer in Dempsey Hill is still the gold standard for delicious, nutritious café fare and gourmet gastro-shopping. Sydney-based interior architects Landini Associates refurbished the airy, cavernous space with a glossy concrete floor, industrial lamps and rows of shiny shelves. These are stacked full of goodies including farmhouse cheeses, olive oils, Italian biscuits and slabs of homemade rocky road. At the weekend it's rammed with shoppers and a loyal contingent of expat Aussies who congregate around the long communal tables for brunch.
Block 9, 1-12 Dempsey Road,
T 6476 1512, www.jonesthegrocer.com

Restaurant André
Fans of chef André Chiang flocked to this
beautiful Chinatown shophouse when he
opened here in 2010. There is artistry
throughout; from the paper-thin plates,
some of which are designed by Chiang
himself, to the signature eight-course
tasting menu melding French nouvelle
cuisine with Mediterranean accents.
41 Bukit Pasoh Road, T 6534 8880,
www.restaurantandre.com

INSIDER'S GUIDE

GEORGE YOUNG, ACTOR

Having ditched a legal career in England, George Young headed east, straight into a life in front of the camera in Singapore. When he's not on set, he's reconnecting with his Asian roots at Master Crab Seafood Restaurant (Block 1-229, 19 Ghim Moh Road, T 6314 1868). 'Bring your appetite,' he advises. In his line of work, Young is frequently on his feet and considers foot reflexology sessions a must. The Green Apple Foot Spa (765 North Bridge Road, T 6299 1555) is a regular haunt: 'It has a cinema room in which you sit back and plug in the headphones while your feet are worked on.'

Young gets his retail fix at The Star Vista mall (1 Vista Exchange Green, T 6694 3111), which has a futuristic atrium and incredible spread of eateries, although the avid gamer can also be found at Funz Centre (5-43/44, 181 Orchard Road, T 6238 6466), browsing the latest computer games. Korean restaurant Joo Mak (4-1 Beauty World Centre, 144 Upper Bukit Timah Road, T 6466 7871) is his preferred dinner destination; he suggests pairing the garlic-fried chicken and barbecued rib-eye with *makgeolli* (rice wine). Young's perfect evening out involves live music by local artists – favoured hangouts are B28 (Basement, The Club Hotel, 28 Ann Siang Road, T 9026 3466), where he enjoys an Old Fashioned and jazz at the weekend, and the rooftop Mad Men Attic Bar (3-2, 11 North Canal Road, T 6222 3529), whose 'entrance is hidden down an alleyway'. *For full addresses, see Resources.*

ARCHITOUR
A GUIDE TO SINGAPORE'S ICONIC BUILDINGS

In their rush to build skyscrapers and fulfil government demands for a modern metropolis, city planners spent the 1970s and 1980s razing whole areas of colonial, Peranakan and art deco buildings. Thankfully, common sense prevailed, resulting in a coordinated effort to preserve Singapore's past while creating next-generation architecture. If the flawlessly renovated colonial-era Baba House (157 Neil Road, T 6227 5731), and Architects 61's reimagining of Frank Dorrington Ward's neoclassical 1933 People's Association HQ (9 King George's Avenue, T 6344 8222) are any indication, it's clear that awareness of the nation's built heritage has been raised.

A scan of the skyline reveals an impressive cocktail of old and new, from bold public housing blocks (see p072), to office towers and modernist classics by SOM, Richard Meier, IM Pei and Kenzo Tange, to Ben van Berkel's 2013 Ardmore Residence (7 Ardmore Park). These will sit alongside grand projects like Zaha Hadid's seven-tower D'Leedon Condo (2015), Ole Scheeren's mixed-use DUO (2017) and Norman Foster's sustainable quarter, Beach Road (2015). Good work is also being done by a younger generation, including Chan Soo Khian, Ko Shiou Hee and WOHA's Wong Mun Summ and Richard Hassell. It's a tricky balancing act between innovation and conservation, but for a city that's always been in a hurry to meet its future, Singapore is rising to the challenge. *For full addresses, see Resources.*

AXA Life Building

There are now more than 700 buildings in the city that top 25 storeys. Many of them are unremarkable for anything except their height, so it's not surprising that very little attention has been paid to Singapore's early, more modest attempts at the high-rise. This 1974 headquarters for the city-state's largest building society, designed by local firm James Ferrie and Partners as the Wing On Life Building, is an understated gem, and at a relatively lowly 64m, it was one of Singapore's first energy-efficient structures. It is now dwarfed by the more contemporary developments on Cecil Street and is easy to miss. As a snapshot of Singapore's doomed flirtation with elegant tropical modernism – all concrete brise-soleil and slimline proportions – it's hard to beat.
150 Cecil Street

Reflections at Keppel Bay

Seen from a distance, Daniel Libeskind's six condominium towers on the edge of Keppel Bay rise up from their forest frontage with a disturbing, shattered, post-apocalyptic quality about them. Up close, the buildings, completed in late 2011 as part of an ongoing development of Keppel Island's southern coastline, bear all the hallmarks of Libeskind's deconstructive bent for asymmetry and odd angles. Displaying hardly any straight lines in their elevations (save for the lift shafts), the towers twist and turn as if they were a stand of willows. Even by Singaporean standards, the scale of Reflections is audacious – 11 low-rise blocks cluster around the base of the trinity of twin towers.
1-33 Keppel Bay View,
www.reflectionsatkeppelbay.com.sg

Stadium MRT

Architects WOHA have been on a roll in Singapore, designing the School of the Arts (T 6338 9663) and the MRT stations Bras Basah – serving the Singapore Art Museum (see p084) – and Stadium, all of which opened in 2010. Of the stations, Stadium MRT has the more intriguing design: the shape evokes a pair of bold, parallel, calligraphic strokes that carve 13m underground. The aluminium-clad crevasse sparkles when the sun shines through a skylight that runs the length of the structure, and the curved form affords extra space in which to accommodate crowds from the adjacent Indoor Stadium (see p090) and National Stadium. WOHA also created the 2007 Newton Suites (60 Newton Road), an eco-friendly condo block that has sky gardens and living walls.
3 Stadium Walk

Church of St Mary of the Angels

In 2003, at a time when many thought that there could be few surprises left on the local architectural scene, WOHA unveiled this beautiful church on the wooded slopes of Bukit Batok. One of the architects' finest works – up there alongside the MRT station designs (see p068) – the church is a graceful meditation on space on a vast scale, and yet it retains an unexpected intimacy. The vaulted eyrie of the main prayer hall is lined with white-oak benches and a forest of giant candelabra, and the light-drenched columbarium (a room with recesses in the walls, where funeral urns are kept) is spectacular. The complex includes 12 reflection pools, a friary, offices and a separate apartment block in which the friars of the parish reside.
5 Bukit Batok East Avenue 2, T 6567 3866, www.stmary.sg

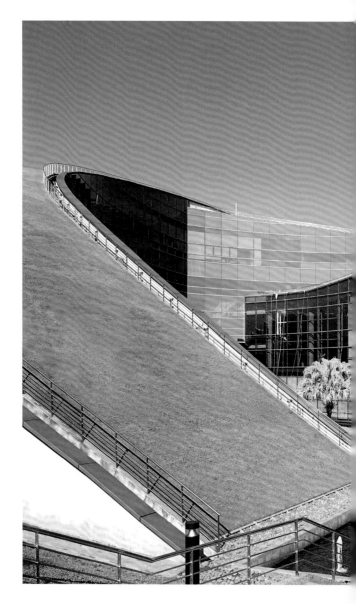

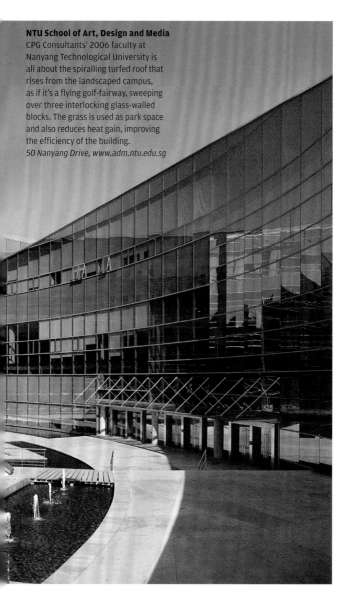

NTU School of Art, Design and Media
CPG Consultants' 2006 faculty at
Nanyang Technological University is
all about the spiralling turfed roof that
rises from the landscaped campus,
as if it's a flying golf-fairway, sweeping
over three interlocking glass-walled
blocks. The grass is used as park space
and also reduces heat gain, improving
the efficiency of the building.
50 Nanyang Drive, www.adm.ntu.edu.sg

Public housing flats
Roughly 80 per cent of the population of Singapore lives in government-subsidised housing, or HDB (Housing and Development Board) flats. The architecture is rather utilitarian, consisting of rows and rows of garishly painted apartments stretching across the urban landscape. Efforts have been made, though, to create imaginative facades, as on this Selegie Road block.

Supreme Court

The city-state's Supreme Court building, just behind its former Palladian digs and across from the squat Parliament House (1 Parliament Place), was Norman Foster's second work in Singapore, completed five years after the 2000 Expo MRT station (21 Changi South Avenue 1). The interiors are suitably lofty – most evident in the central atrium (opposite) – and they call to mind London's Canary Wharf station. The Court of Appeal, the country's highest judicial authority, sits in a Starship Enterprise-like dome (above), which, like the cupola of Foster's Reichstag in Berlin, incorporates a wraparound viewing platform. Opinion is split between those who deride the sci-fi form and others who are thrilled to have yet another Foster design on the island. *1 Supreme Court Lane, T 6336 0644, www.supremecourt.gov.sg*

Assyafaah Mosque
In many ways, Forum Architects' mosque
defies convention. There isn't a dome in
sight, and slight screens blur the interior/
exterior divide; carved with symbolic
tracery, they double as shade and
ventilation. The prayer hall (pictured)
is the building's grandest statement:
a four-storey slanted white marble wall,
inscribed with Koranic script.
1 Admiralty Lane, T 6756 3008

Marina Bay Sands/Helix Bridge
Moshe Safdie's resort dominates Marina
Bay. The three towers are conjoined by a
cantilevered 12,400 sq m roof garden (see
p038) and resemble a giant three-legged
pi. The 280m-long Helix Bridge, by Cox
Architecture, Arup and Architects 61, gives
pedestrian access, its steel bands twisting
in opposite directions as if a strand of DNA.
10 Bayfront Avenue, T 6688 8868,
www.marinabaysands.com

SHOPPING

THE BEST RETAIL THERAPY AND WHAT TO BUY

There was a time when shopping here was confined to the glossy stores on the Orchard Road belt, and the selection was limited to clothing, accessories and electronics. These days, the choice is more sophisticated. Discouraged by high rents, retailers have forsaken the strip for settings such as Purvis Street and Ann Siang Hill, whereas the shops of Club Street, Haji Lane and their arterial roads are luring the fashion conscious thanks to good designs by local talent, alongside leading labels from Tokyo and New York.

Little India and Chinatown are havens for Old Asia antiques. Electronic bargains can be sourced at Funan DigitalLife Mall (109 North Bridge Road, T 6336 8327) or Peninsula Plaza (111 North Bridge Road, T 6337 4274), but prepare to haggle. Mega-malls are also alive and well. The new crop is led by ION (see p010), Bugis Junction (200 Victoria Street, T 6557 6557) and Central (6 Eu Tong Sen Street, T 6532 9922), while the city's first luxury concept store, The Hour Glass Malmaison (1-1 Knightsbridge, 270 Orchard Road, T 6884 8484), opened in 2011. It is possible to find an independent gem, such as Hansel (2-14 Mandarin Gallery, 333a Orchard Road, T 6836 5367), which sells owner Jo Soh's womenswear collection; Rockstar (Ground floor, 22 Orchard Road, T 6883 2309), stocking everything from footwear to fragrance; and BooksActually (9 Yong Siak Street, T 6222 9195), which offers tomes by local authors. *For full addresses, see Resources.*

Lorgan's The Retro Store

Owner Lorgan Wong is an unabashed retro-design hound. Entering this kitsch, rambling store in an industrial park is a little like stumbling across Ali Baba's cave, albeit one stuck in an altogether different time warp. Thanks to Wong's regular sorties to Australia and Europe, shoppers can expect to find surprising treasures from the 1930s to the 1970s, including well-priced reupholstered furniture, vintage clothes and lava lamps. Depending on your luck, you may uncover pieces by Poul Kjærholm, Pierre Paulin or Eero Aarnio. One of our visits yielded a pristine Artifort 'Oyster' chair. Sticking to its philosophy of 'design within reach', Lorgan's stocks a range of reproduction designer Scandinavian furniture.

1-3 Century Warehouse, 100e Pasir Panjang Road, T 6272 4988, www.lorgans.com

Salon by Surrender
Probably Singapore's most striking
multi-label unisex boutique, this store,
opened in 2013, has shaken up the
often staid local fashion scene. Inspired
by 18th-century European tearooms,
the black-and-white marbled space
stocks the likes of Head Porter, Arts &
Science, and Maison Martin Margiela.
B2-232/233, 2 Bayfront Avenue,
The Shoppes at Marina Bay Sands

Supermama

When Edwin Low, Supermama's creative director, asked five local design studios to contribute to Singapore Icons, a range of ceramics that paid homage to everyday Singaporean life, he couldn't have guessed how popular it would be, especially among homesick expats abroad. The images, fired on to blue-and-white saucers, plates and chopstick stands produced by Japanese porcelain makers Kihara, resemble much-loved symbols. Examples include HDB by Chang Shian Wei (a stylised silhouette of public-housing balconies), or the National Bird of Singapore by Relay Room (above). The ceramics can be purchased from the Supermama store at SAM at 8Q (opposite; T 6332 3222), but it's also worth a trip to Low's studio (30a Seah Street) to see what other tricks he has up his sleeve. *www.supermama.sg*

PACT

Part of the wave of new concept stores in Singapore, PACT is a funky triumvirate of restaurant, retailer and hair salon. It opened in 2012 and caters to young urban hipsters who prefer a closet with more indie cred. The store, KIN (right), offers an edgy selection of fashion, mostly from local labels such as Sifr (www.sifrsite.com), although some European and American brands can also be found here; the Robert Geller tracksuits and Monitaly cardigans are a particular hit. The restaurant, Kilo (T 6884 7560), is set inside a sparsely decorated space, the perfect backdrop for its restrained Japanese-Vietnamese menu. Topping this trinity is PACT+LIM (T 6884 4143), the city's flagship of the Japanese salon chain, Less Is More.
2-16/17/18/19 Orchard Central,
181 Orchard Road, T 6238 6362,
www.visitpact.com

SPORTS AND SPAS

WORK OUT, CHILL OUT OR JUST WATCH

You wouldn't have thought that Singaporeans were a sporty lot but during the FIFA World Cup crowds gather around TV sets in pubs, bars and hawker centres across the island. Now a fixture on the F1 calendar and host of the WTA Tour Championships, the city has achieved international recognition, if not for its sporting prowess then for its facilities, including the new National Stadium (1 Stadium Drive, T 6344 2660), completed in 2014. Indeed, the sheer number of swimming pools, stadiums and gyms, brushed-steel and air-conditioned to the last, is surprising. Perhaps this has something to do with the compulsory two-year national service for men, or because an overwhelming majority of the population lives in high-rises, and so loves to exercise either in a park – Fort Canning is popular – or one of the excellent public pools, such as Katong Swimming Complex (111 Wilkinson Road, T 6344 9609). The entry fees are a pittance, the feel is charmingly retro and the layout is a reminder that good, functional design never dates.

Most of the island's roads tend to be choked with traffic, which explains why the Botanic Gardens (1 Cluny Road, T 6471 7138) and Mount Faber Park (opposite) are a refuge for joggers. The setting of East Coast Park has plenty to offer canoeists, windsurfers and cyclists, whereas Marina Country Club (600 Ponggol Seventeenth Avenue, T 6385 6166) is a haven for wakeboarders and waterskiers. For full addresses, see Resources.

Henderson Waves

Singaporeans, never mind tourists, still think of their city as one giant glitzy mall-and-dining destination. Less known are the island's green spaces, especially the rainforest and mangrove swamps found in the centre, west and north. The National Parks Board has built a first-class network of walkways and bridges; a glorious jogging route. The Southern Ridges is a 10km trail through the parks of Kent Ridge, Mount Faber and Telok Blangah Hill. It crosses Henderson Waves, a 274m-long, 36m-high, snake-like pedestrian bridge. Designed by architects RSP using yellow bakau wood for the decking, the tops of the nine 'waves' form alcoves from which you can take in the view. The bridge itself is a fine sight at night, when it is illuminated by LEDs. *Mount Faber Park/Telok Blangah Hill Park, www.nparks.gov.sg*

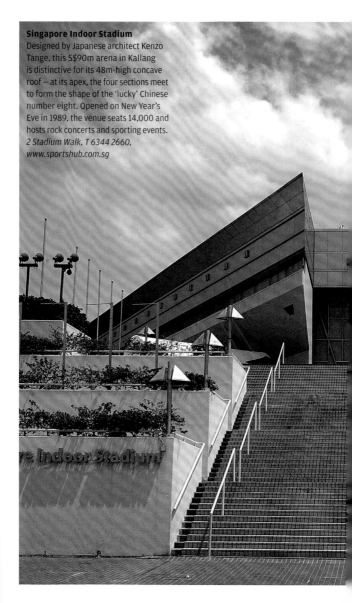

Singapore Indoor Stadium
Designed by Japanese architect Kenzo Tange, this S$90m arena in Kallang is distinctive for its 48m-high concave roof – at its apex, the four sections meet to form the shape of the 'lucky' Chinese number eight. Opened on New Year's Eve in 1989, the venue seats 14,000 and hosts rock concerts and sporting events.
2 Stadium Walk, T 6344 2660,
www.sportshub.com.sg

Banyan Tree Spa

There's nothing like the frisson of having a facial and a steam in a facility that floats 55 storeys above street level. This 1,213 sq m day spa is the first in the city from the Banyan Tree, the Singapore-based luxury hotel group. An earth-toned space swathed in hand-carved timber panels, travertine, stone and onyx, it's a welcome retreat from the heat outside. Each of the 15 treatment rooms has vertiginous views of skyscrapers and across Marina Bay. A crack team of therapists, each trained at the Banyan Tree's own academy, adroitly oversee Tropical Rainmist experiences (a hybrid rain shower and steam bath), Hawaiian Lomi Lomi massages and Royal Banyan muscle rubs with steamed herbal pouches soaked in sesame seed oil.
Level 55, Tower 1, 10 Bayfront Avenue, T 6688 8825, www.banyantreespa.com

Beauty Emporium at House

The template for Beauty Emporium is an upmarket grocery and, indeed, the 1,580 sq m space (part of the Spa Esprit empire) is how Whole Foods Market may look, feel and smell if it specialised in beauty products. Customers push bijoux trolleys across concrete floors that are covered with wooden crates full of lotions and potions from Malin+Goetz, REN and SCO. There's also a florist and a section where a changing roster of retailers sell their wares. Head to the Strip mani and pedi area (above), or a treatment room for a circulation-boosting House Proud massage using pepper and ginger (S$128 per hour); a Back to Balance massage with doTERRA oils (S$235); or a facial using organic Ilcsi products (from S$160 per hour).
Dempsey House, 8d Dempsey Road, T 6475 0070, www.dempseyhill.com

Fitness First Platinum

It's difficult to imagine how anyone could get a workout done when the view is like this. Even from the fifth floor of this Raffles Place skyscraper, designed by Skidmore, Owings & Merrill, the panorama across Marina Bay is stunning. Clocking in at 930 sq m, the gym, which was refurbished in 2012, boasts state-of-the-art cardio equipment complete with audio and visual entertainment, a large group-exercise studio, a sauna, a steam bath and a covered sky garden, and can provide complimentary kit. Aquafit exercise classes are held in the outdoor 25m heated lap pool (above), which looks out over the Singapore River and the Esplanade theatre complex. Odd, though, that a gym also offers movie rentals.

5-1 One George Street, 1 George Street, T 6538 7666, www.fitnessfirst.com.sg

ESCAPES

WHERE TO GO IF YOU WANT TO LEAVE TOWN

Singapore's location at the heart of South-East Asia makes it easy to depart for a quick change of scenery. For instance, Phnom Penh is kicking off the emotional shackles of its troubled past with an exciting combination of smart restaurants, contemporary art and film festivals, against a landscape of beautifully restored colonial architecture and a riverfront flecked with seagulls. It also helps that price wars between the budget airlines have spilled over to the bigger boys' territory – these days it is not uncommon to find newspaper adverts for S$20 return flights to Phuket.

As so many destinations are only an hour or two away by plane, choices are innumerable. Short breaks are tempting all over the region – from Bali (see p102), whose many-splendoured charms include the eco-friendly Alila Villas Soori (Banjar Dukuh, Desa Kelating, T +62 361 894 6388), to Kuala Lumpur and its bustling nightlife and insanely good food. Many well-heeled locals have built weekend getaways in Phuket, whereas others, armed with a strong Singaporean dollar, nip north to Bangkok, or further afield to Tokyo and Seoul, for retail therapy and a fix of the local cuisine. But while packing your other Wallpaper* City Guides into your overnight bag, don't forget there are some great destinations in Singapore itself, such as the islands of Pulau Ubin (see p103) and Kusu – both worthy excursions, even if it's just for the day.
For full addresses, see Resources.

Bandar Seri Begawan, Brunei

Seat of one of the world's longest-standing absolute monarchies, Brunei is a two-hour flight away. The most significant event in its history was the discovery of oil in 1929, and liquid gold has lubricated Brunei's economy ever since, allowing this nation, whose population is little more than 400,000, to call its own shots. Fans of architectural excess will thrill to the 'monarchuments' that dot the country, such as Bandar Seri Begawan's Sultan Omar Ali Saifuddien Mosque (above), and the Crystal Arch (overleaf), a seven-tonne replica of a diamond ring that the sultan presented to his first wife. Live like a king yourself by checking into the capital's Empire Hotel & Country Club (T +673 241 8888), which has 24-carat gold-leaf detailing, an 80m-high atrium and no fewer than eight swimming pools.

Crystal Arch, Bandar Seri Begawan, Brunei

Macalister Mansion, Penang

This little island in north-west Malaysia, an 85-minute plane ride from Singapore, is undergoing a renaissance. Long famed for its incredible food, it's crowded with attractive British colonial architecture, Buddhist temples and, today, a clutch of hipster hotels. Book into the Macalister Mansion, which launched in 2012. This former governor's residence is a grand fin de siècle pile that was given a facelift by Colin Seah of Ministry of Design. While sympathetically preserving the original features, Seah has given each room a unique look, be it via sculptural art, as in Room 1 (above), chrome canopies or iron spiral staircases. The Living Room (opposite) offers a casual space for dining without scrimping on the flavours.

228 Macalister Road, George Town, T +60 4228 3888, www.macalistermansion.com

Alila Villas Uluwatu, Bali

Bali is a hugely popular destination for Singaporeans. New resorts now scramble for limited waterfront views, but Alila Villas Uluwatu has secured the perfect location on a limestone plateau on Bali's southern tip. Eco-friendly features have been installed throughout the 14-hectare resort, including water-recycling systems, and creature comforts are legion. The 86 villas, each with its own pool and private cabana (one-bedroom, above), feature volcanic-stone and bamboo ceilings, as well as organic toiletries that are made locally using mandarin and lemongrass. In 2014, the Alila group opened Seminyak (T 6735 8300), a 240-room resort sited on the island's south-western coast. *Jalan Belimbing Sari, Banjar Tambiyak, Desa Pecatu, T +62 361 848 2166, www.alilahotels.com/uluwatu*

Pulau Ubin

For a sense of what Singapore looked like 100 years ago, Pulau Ubin fits the bill handsomely. The island used to be five smaller islets that were united by bunds built for prawn farming, and its name, which translates as 'tile island', is taken from the granite that was mined here until the 1960s. These days, the disused quarries are lakes, and you'll also find dense emerald forest, rubber plantations, prawn farms and fishing villages. The cool, damp gloom of the mangrove swamps is home to flying foxes, lumbering monitor lizards and crested goshawks, while carnivorous pitcher plants and wild orchids bloom in the shade of the rubber trees. Pulau Ubin is a 10-minute 'bumboat' ride from Singapore; depart from Changi Point Ferry Terminal at Changi Village.

NOTES

SKETCHES AND MEMOS

RESOURCES
CITY GUIDE DIRECTORY

HOTELS

ADDRESSES AND ROOM RATES

Alila Seminyak 102
  Room rates:
  prices on request
  Jalan Taman Ganesha 9
  Petitenget
  Kerobokan
  Bali
  T 6735 8300
  www.alilahotels.com/seminyak

Alila Villas Soori 096
  Room rates:
  villa, from S$625
  Banjar Dukuh
  Desa Kelating
  Kerambitan
  Tabanan
  Bali
  T +62 361 894 6388
  www.alilahotels.com/soori

Alila Villas Uluwatu 102
  Room rates:
  villa, from S$730
  Jalan Belimbing Sari
  Banjar Tambiyak
  Desa Pecatu
  Bali
  T +62 361 848 2166
  www.alilahotels.com/uluwatu

Capella 017
  Room rates:
  double, from S$710;
  Premier Seaview Room 410, S$760;
  Colonial Manor, S$10,000
  1 The Knolls
  Sentosa Island
  T 6377 8888
  www.capellasingapore.com

The Club 016
  Room rates:
  double, from S$235
  28 Ann Siang Road
  T 6808 2188
  www.theclub.com.sg

The Empire Hotel & Country Club 097
  Room rates:
  double, from S$320
  Jerudong BG3122
  Negara Brunei Darussalam
  Bandar Seri Begawan
  Brunei
  T +673 241 8888
  www.theempirehotel.com

Hotel Fort Canning 016
  Room rates:
  double, from S$550
  11 Canning Walk
  T 6559 6769
  www.hfcsingapore.com

Four Seasons 028
  Room rates:
  double, from S$420;
  Executive Suite, from S$610;
  Room 1603, from S$880
  190 Orchard Boulevard
  T 6734 1110
  www.fourseasons.com/singapore

The Fullerton Bay Hotel 016
  Room rates:
  double, from S$685
  80 Collyer Quay
  T 6333 8388
  www.fullertonbayhotel.com

Macalister Mansion 100
 Room rates:
 double, from S$290;
 Room 1, S$405
 228 Macalister Road
 George Town
 Penang
 Malaysia
 T +60 4228 3888
 www.macalistermansion.com
Marina Bay Sands 016
 Room rates:
 double, from S$350
 10 Bayfront Avenue
 T 6688 8868
 www.marinabaysands.com
Moon 026
 Room rates:
 double, from S$175;
 Moonlight Suite, from S$455
 23 Dickson Road
 T 6827 6666
 www.moon.com.sg
Naumi Liora 030
 Room rates:
 double, from S$380;
 Liora Porch, S$580
 55 Keong Saik Road
 T 6922 9000
 www.naumiliora.com
New Majestic Hotel 024
 Room rates:
 double, from S$270;
 Premier Garden Room, S$300;
 Attic Suite, from S$430
 31-37 Bukit Pasoh Road
 T 6511 4700
 www.newmajestichotel.com

Parkroyal on Pickering 018
 Room rates:
 double, from S$300
 3 Upper Pickering Street
 T 6809 8888
 www.parkroyalhotels.com
Raffles 016
 Room rates:
 double, S$1,400
 1 Beach Road
 T 6337 1886
 www.raffles.com
Regent 022
 Room rates:
 double, from S$275;
 Room 1133, from S$430
 1 Cuscaden Road
 T 6733 8888
 www.regenthotels.com/singapore
The Ritz-Carlton Millenia 020
 Room rates:
 double, from S$1,015;
 Premier Suite 3126, from S$1,340
 7 Raffles Avenue
 T 6337 8888
 www.ritzcarlton.com
St Regis 016
 Room rates:
 double, from S$900
 29 Tanglin Road
 T 6506 6888
 www.starwoodhotels.com/stregis
Shangri-La 016
 Room rates:
 double, from S$575
 22 Orange Grove Road
 T 6737 3644
 www.shangri-la.com

Sofitel So 016
  Room rates:
  double, from S$490
  35 Robinson Road
  www.sofitel.com
TreeTop Lofts 016
  Room rates:
  double, from S$3,000
  Resorts World Sentosa
  8 Sentosa Gateway
  T 6577 8899
  www.rwsentosa.com
W 016
  Room rates:
  double, from S$430
  21 Ocean Way
  T 6808 7288
  www.wsingaporesentosacove.com
Wanderlust 016
  Room rates:
  double, from S$300
  2 Dickson Road
  T 6396 3322
  www.wanderlusthotel.com
Wangz Hotel 016
  Room rates:
  double, from S$500
  231 Outram Road
  T 6595 1388
  www.wangzhotel.com
Westin 016
  Room rates:
  double, from S$345
  12 Marina View
  Asia Square Tower
  T 6922 6888
  www.starwoodhotels.com/singapore

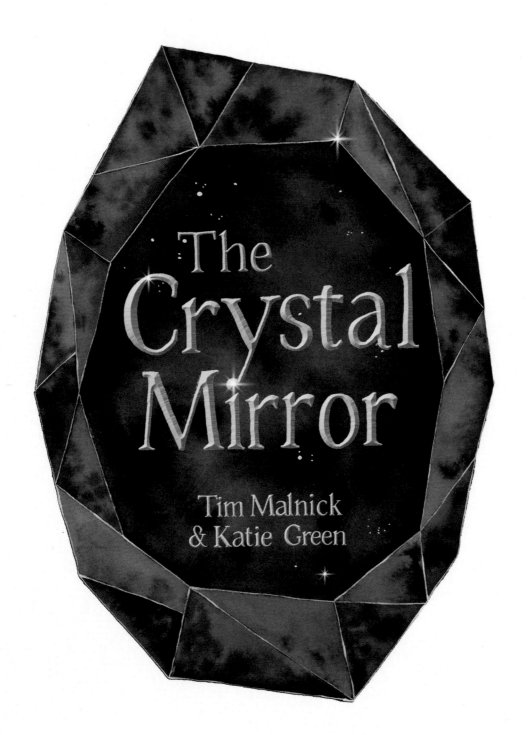

The Crystal Mirror

Tim Malnick
& Katie Green

Vala

First published in 2013 by Vala Publishing Co-operative
Text © Tim Malnick 2013
Illustration © Katie Green 2013

Vala Publishing Co-operative Ltd
8 Gladstone Street, Bristol, BS3 3AY, UK
For further information on Vala publications, see
www.valapublishers.coop or write to info@valapublishers.coop

Typeset in Freya, designed by Saku Heinänen
Printed and bound in the UK by CPI Colour

A CIP catalogue record for this title is available from
the British Library.
ISBN 978-1-908363-09-1

For Noah
& Elliot

The Cuddliest Monster in the World

The Master Painter

Polly, the
Girl Who Was
Always
Changing

The Story of
Oswald Bat

The
Rainbow Bridge
of the Sea

The Cuddliest Monster in the World

In a cave, on top of a hill, overlooking a lush, green forest, there lived the cuddliest monster in the world. The cuddliest monster in the world was seven foot tall and covered from head to toe in the most luxuriant, soft, brown, shaggy fur, which was so soft that anyone who felt it would want to bury their face in it, or curl up inside and fall asleep. He had sharp, pointy teeth, which would have looked extremely fierce and frightening if it weren't for the fact that he was always wearing the most charming and rather cheeky grin. The cuddliest monster in the world also had a big, boomy voice, which could certainly have been most scary and deafening, were it not that however loud he rumbled and whatever he bellowed, there was always, somehow, a feeling of complete gentleness and kindness. The cuddliest monster in the world lived alone, quite happily, in his cave on top of the hill. He spent his days growing vegetables and flowers in his garden, making up tunes on his favourite flute and sipping tea as he gazed out on the world around him.

One day there emerged from the forest a mighty warrior, carrying a gleaming sword. He appeared to be heading for the cave. Now, this warrior was brave and strong and many, many years ago he had taken a solemn vow and sworn to kill every monster in the whole world. He had spent long years travelling from place to place, killing monsters everywhere with his sharp sword.

To tell the truth, he couldn't quite remember any more exactly why he had started out on this quest in the first place – perhaps it had seemed like a good idea at the time. And the

strange thing was that every time he killed one monster, thinking that surely this was the last one and that he could at last relax, the warrior heard of another monster and then another, suddenly appearing out of nowhere. Of course he would then dash off to kill it, only to find that yet another would soon emerge to take its place. So, as the mighty warrior climbed the hill on that particular day to slay the cuddliest monster in the world, he was feeling, to say the least, a little weary and disenchanted with this lifelong quest of his.

The cuddliest monster in the world was at that moment sitting down by the fire after a good morning's gardening, waiting for the kettle to boil. As he saw this distant figure striding up the hill towards him, he was rather pleased at the thought of some company and someone to share his tea with, on what was turning out to be a beautiful morning.

"Hello there!" he called out, his deep, boomy voice echoing around the valley and making a few small stones begin to shake.

"Greetings, monster!" cried the warrior. "Prepare to meet your death. For I have vowed to kill all the monsters in the world and so today I must kill you!"

Well, this might have ruined quite a lot of people's day, but not, it appears, the cuddliest monster's.

"Wouldn't you rather have some tea?" he roared sweetly.

The warrior was indeed surprised by this remark, and for a brief second the thought of sitting and drinking some tea instead of chopping the monster's head off did seem extremely appealing. But he could not forget his vow, even if he had forgotten why he had made it in the first place.

"No, monster, I must kill you," he declared. "Prepare to die!"

Whether or not the monster was trying to look fierce at that moment I'm not sure, but there was still, as always, more than a hint of a grin on his lips. Once again his deep, gentle voice rang out.

"Oh well. If you must, I suppose. But," he added, "it hardly seems fair. After all, you've got that big sharp sword and by the looks of you I'm not the first monster you've fought and I'm rather unfit and not used to fighting at all. And I've not yet had my lunch. Wouldn't it be fairer and more fun for you if you put down your sword and we wrestled, man to monster, so to speak?"

The warrior thought about this. He had to admit that the fights had been getting too easy lately. He could do with a challenge.

"Very well," he shouted, laying down his sword, "we will wrestle to the death." And with a mighty yell he ran up the hill and threw himself with all his might towards the monster, gripping him in a powerful bear hug. The warrior had his arms around the monster and was straining and struggling, gulping and grimacing. As he was doing all this, the monster very gently put his arms around the warrior and just held him there.

"Grrgghhhhhh!!" groaned the warrior, using every bit of his strength to try to squeeze the breath out of the monster, to throw him to the floor or crush his ribs.

The monster just continued to hold his arms gently around the warrior.

"Agghgrrgh!!!!" grunted the warrior, every muscle bursting as he tried desperately to defeat his foe. And still the monster just stood there breathing softly, a grin across his razor sharp teeth, holding the warrior gently with his huge, furry arms.

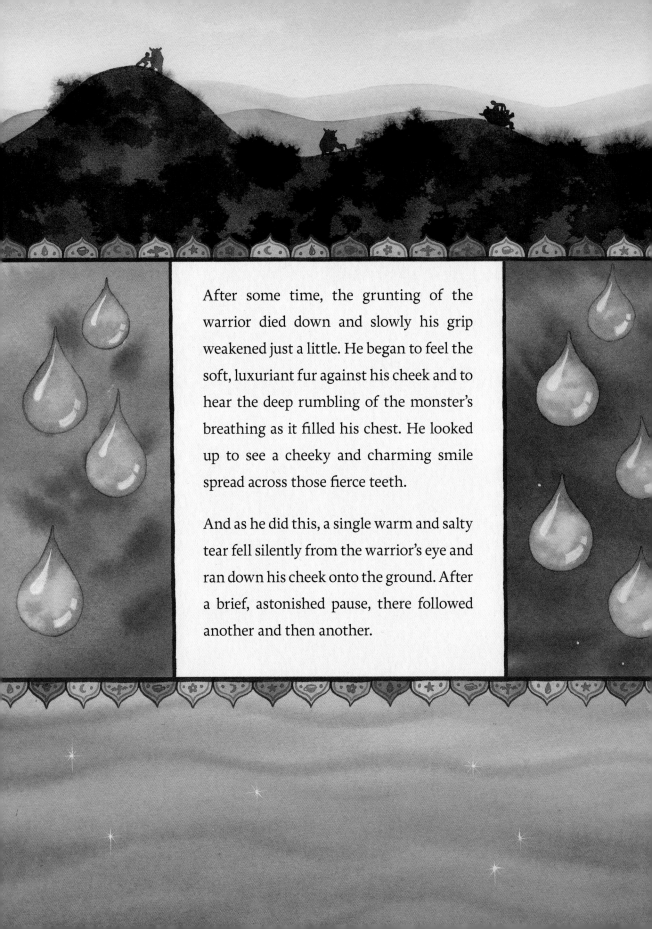

After some time, the grunting of the warrior died down and slowly his grip weakened just a little. He began to feel the soft, luxuriant fur against his cheek and to hear the deep rumbling of the monster's breathing as it filled his chest. He looked up to see a cheeky and charming smile spread across those fierce teeth.

And as he did this, a single warm and salty tear fell silently from the warrior's eye and ran down his cheek onto the ground. After a brief, astonished pause, there followed another and then another.

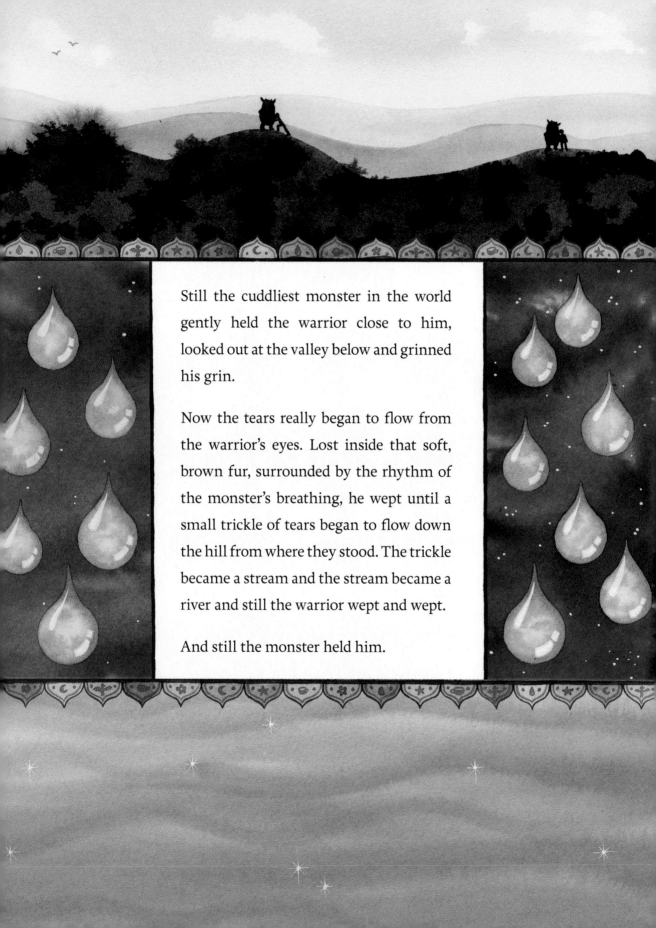

Still the cuddliest monster in the world gently held the warrior close to him, looked out at the valley below and grinned his grin.

Now the tears really began to flow from the warrior's eyes. Lost inside that soft, brown fur, surrounded by the rhythm of the monster's breathing, he wept until a small trickle of tears began to flow down the hill from where they stood. The trickle became a stream and the stream became a river and still the warrior wept and wept.

And still the monster held him.

No one knows how long it was before the warrior looked up again. It was night, and a thousand stars were shining in the clear sky all around them. Now, in place of the monster's breathing, the warrior could hear the gurgling and rushing of a mighty river that flowed from where they stood down the hill and into the forest below. As he looked up, he saw that his tears had become a torrent of diamonds and silver in the darkness of the night.

And at last, the warrior silently took off his armour and left his sword where it lay. Gently bowing to the cuddliest monster in the world, his hardest and softest opponent, his kindest and undefeated foe, he walked down the hill and followed the river into the forest.

There for the rest of his life he lived in peace, surrounded by the plants and the creatures of the forest. He built a boat, so that once in a while he could carry those who wished to go across his river of diamonds and silver and tears.

And once or twice a week he would walk up the hill to visit his most excellent friend, the cuddliest monster in the world. They would talk and talk and look out at the world and drink what, of course, turned out to be extremely good tea.

The Master Painter

Once there lived a master painter and he was a very fine and wonderful painter indeed. For he painted whatever he saw in the world, and what he saw in the world was beautiful. Wherever he looked, whatever he saw, he saw its beauty and he painted it. That was his gift and he accepted it gladly.

One day the king summoned the master painter to his palace and commanded him to paint his portrait. Now the king was not particularly good or kind, nor was he particularly handsome. But the master painter looked beyond the king's lust for power, beyond his greed, insensitivity and ugliness, to the beauty that he saw in everybody and everything. So that was what he painted.

When the master painter had finished and left the palace, the king looked at the picture. He was outraged. All he could see as he looked at the canvas was an ugly, spiteful, fearful and greedy man staring back at him, and he was deeply insulted. "Treason," he muttered to himself, "infamy, sedition, heresy, how dare he!" The man would have to pay and pay dearly for his insolence.

So a few days later the king once more summoned the master painter to his palace.

"Master Painter," said the king, once the painter had paid his respects, "I have seen the portrait you painted of me and now it is time for you to collect your reward. You will follow my lord chamberlain and he will show you how I have chosen to repay you for your work."

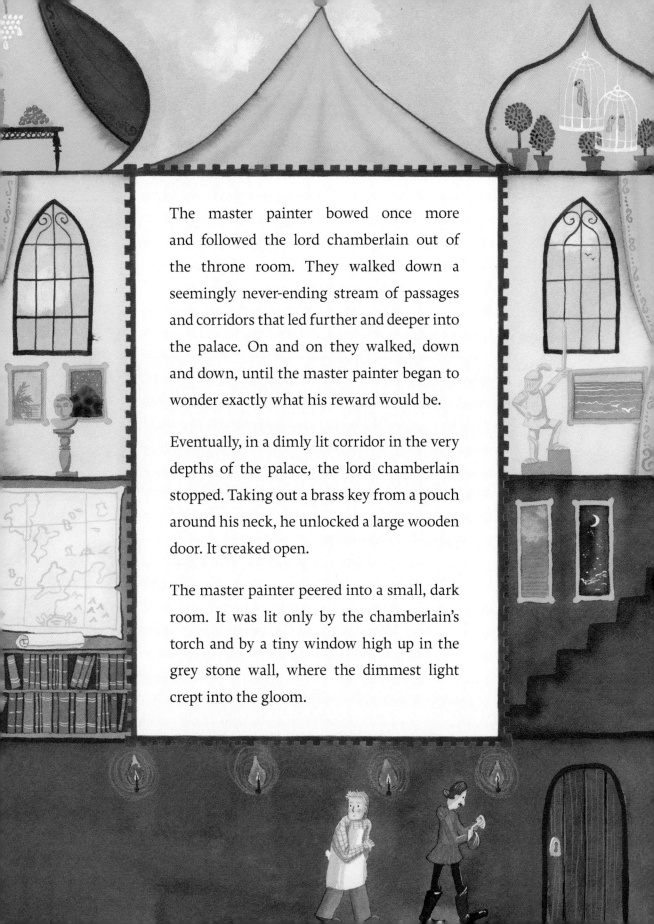

The master painter bowed once more and followed the lord chamberlain out of the throne room. They walked down a seemingly never-ending stream of passages and corridors that led further and deeper into the palace. On and on they walked, down and down, until the master painter began to wonder exactly what his reward would be.

Eventually, in a dimly lit corridor in the very depths of the palace, the lord chamberlain stopped. Taking out a brass key from a pouch around his neck, he unlocked a large wooden door. It creaked open.

The master painter peered into a small, dark room. It was lit only by the chamberlain's torch and by a tiny window high up in the grey stone wall, where the dimmest light crept into the gloom.

In the middle of the otherwise totally bare and empty room, the master painter saw the most amazing sight. There was a finely crafted easel on which was stretched a thick, blank canvas. Laid out around the easel was a collection of the most wonderful paints and brushes he had ever seen. There were a thousand colours of the purest pigments and inks, rich charcoals and pastels, brushes with the softest and most luxurious bristles, pencils sharp and precise, rounded and thick. There was every possible painting material he could ever have wished for.

In rapture he spent many minutes examining this wonderful gift. When finally he could speak once more he said, "I am honoured, Lord Chamberlain, I do not feel I am worthy of such a gift as this."

"Oh, but indeed you are, Master Painter," said the chamberlain, and without warning he slammed the door shut and locked it behind him. The master painter was left alone with just the paints and the single blank canvas in the otherwise bare and empty room. The dim, grey light crept through the tiny window high, high up in the wall.

And then he heard the voice of the king. "You dared to paint me as ugly, you dared to insult me with what you saw. So now you will live forever with a thousand paints and brushes but never again will you see the world."

So the master painter lived in that small, bare room with a thousand fine paints and brushes but just a dull, faint grey light creeping night and day through the window high, high up. Once a day, food and water were pushed through an opening in the door, but from that day onwards he saw and heard no one, nothing. And all was grey.

First he painted from his memory. On that first day on the single canvas he painted what he knew of the world and its beauty. He painted the sky with clouds and sun, snow and rain, and the hills with sharp rocks and sparkling streams. He painted trees and plants, young and green and old and bare. Animals large and small, in the air, on the land and in the water, the hunting and the hunted. He painted men and women, newborn babies, children, the old and the dying. He painted them at work and at play, in joy and sorrow. On that single canvas he painted what he knew of the world and its beauty.

When he awoke the next day to greyness once more, the painting was gone and a single new blank canvas was in its place.

For many months, even years, the master painter painted what he knew of the world and its beauty. He painted his friends and his enemies, his lovers and family, places he knew well and those he'd just passed through. He painted animals and flowers, land and sea. And each morning, when he awoke, his painting was gone and in its place was a new, blank canvas and the same ever-present, unchanging, unrelenting greyness.

Slowly, gradually, in that all-pervading dullness, the master painter began to forget the beauty of the world.

Then he painted pictures of the room he was in, empty and dull though it was. He painted pictures of the bare stone walls from every angle, the single tiny window high, high up. He painted pictures of the bread and water that arrived each day and of the paints and the pencils and many images of his own body. For weeks he painted portraits of a cockroach that had crawled into the room and died. He painted its beauty as it turned slowly to dust in the gloom.

But slowly, slowly, all that too became lost and grey and each day his painting was replaced by a single blank canvas. The king was starving him of the world and of its beauty. Something inside him was being suffocated, moment by moment, hour by hour, day by day. And some days now he did not paint at all. He could not paint.

As he forgot the world and the room around him became an unfathomable greyness, the master painter began to paint his dreams. He yearned each day for sleep so that it might bring him a memory plucked from nowhere, a forgotten face, a strange beast. Now when he could paint, he painted angels and devils, gods and demons, impossible places. He painted the lives of people long ago and those still to come, far, far away and yet all within him. But slowly, slowly, after many months and years, even these faded to grey.

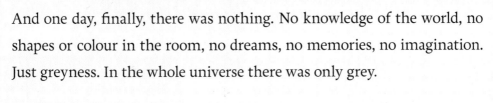

And one day, finally, there was nothing. No knowledge of the world, no shapes or colour in the room, no dreams, no memories, no imagination. Just greyness. In the whole universe there was only grey.

The king had starved him of the world and its beauty. Something inside was suffocated.

That night the master painter lay once more on the floor to sleep, his canvas covered with dust and blank now as it had been seemingly for ever. And he knew, "This is the last time I will lay down to sleep in this room."

Dreams were long forgotten to the master painter, and as he slept he was within greyness, the same all-pervading gloom. In sleep and waking always the same.

And then. Somewhere in the greyness he saw a tiny spark of light far off. A speck of brightness almost impossibly faint and yet strong enough to call to him from afar. As he turned towards it, it seemed to flicker just a fraction, a little brighter, a little bolder. In his dream, as the master painter began to walk towards the light, it grew brighter still, just a touch, in the immense greyness that was all around. And now he walked, ran, stumbling madly towards this flickering light and after hours or centuries or perhaps only a few seconds, he came to the light and saw that it was a flame. A single flame alight in a universe of grey.

The master painter bent down. As he peered into the single flame, he saw once again the world as he knew it. After so many years it was as he always knew it had been, so strangely familiar, so mysteriously obvious. And he knew what he must do.

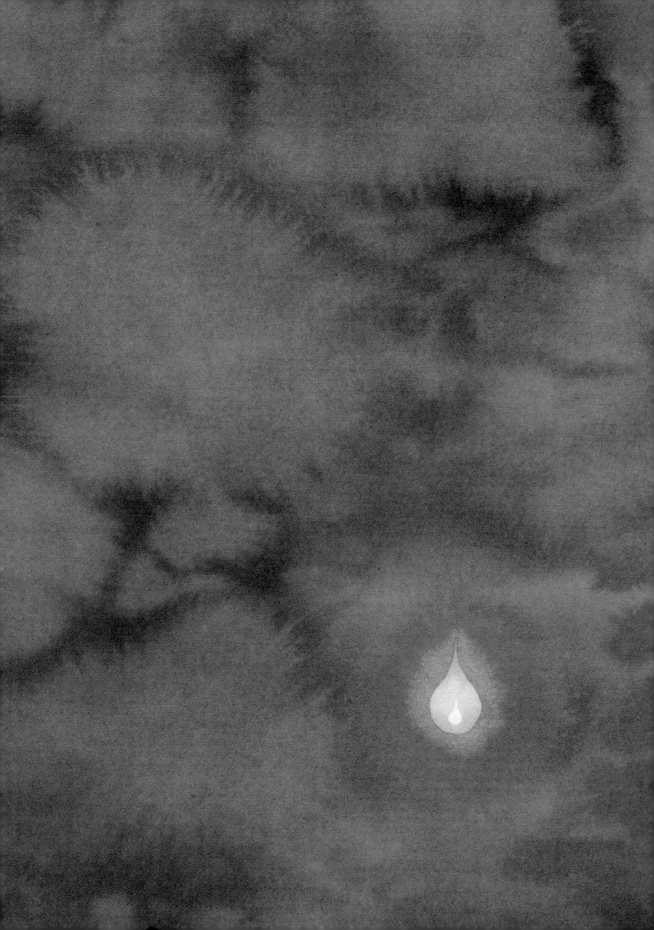

Awake or still dreaming, the difference was unclear to him, the master painter gently took the blank canvas from the dust-covered easel and tore it into pieces. And he took his thousand paints and brushes and he painted what he had seen onto the walls all around him and on the floor and on the ceiling and the door.

All around him he painted the sky with clouds and sun, snow and rain, and the hills with sharp rocks and sparkling streams. He painted trees and plants, young and green and old and bare. Animals large and small, in the air, on the land and in the water, the hunting and the hunted. He painted men and women, newborn babies, children, the old and the dying. He painted them at work and at play, in joy and sorrow. On the walls around him the master painter painted what he knew of the world and its beauty.

And now he looked
down at the soft grass and
wild flowers he had painted
beneath his feet, put down his
brush, and turning towards the
distant mountains, the master
painter left the room forever.

Polly, the Girl Who Was Always Changing

In a light, white room, behind clean, cotton curtains, on the busiest street in the busiest town in a particular sunny, dusty country, lived a young girl called Polly, with eyes as bright as a full moon and deep as the sea. Polly was beautiful and wise and caring. But for all that she was, she did not feel happy. Every day she would look out from behind her curtains at the people passing by as they went about their lives in the street below.

"See that greengrocer," she would think, "he knows exactly where to pitch his stall and exactly what to charge for each of his coloured fruits and vegetables. And he knows exactly what to say, for otherwise he would not be able to shout out so loud for everyone in the market to hear."

"See that soldier," she would say to herself, "marching off to some distant land. He knows exactly where he is going and is never out of step. And his uniform is so smart and tidy because he knows just what to wear and how to wear it. And he knows just which orders to give and which to follow. You can see it by the gleam in his eye."

"And see that mother with her children," Polly would sigh, "every moment she is thinking of them and looking after them. She knows just what she must do to get them food, and keep them safe and out of trouble. And although they are mischievous they follow her every word because they know she does just what is necessary."

You see, for all that she was, Polly felt that she was never the same and was always changing from one moment to the next, so she never really knew who exactly she was. Like the moon, which grows out of darkness to become a silver splinter and then a big, round, glowing sphere before it slowly fades away again, so she would feel sometimes big, sometimes small, sometimes in-between and sometimes almost as though she wasn't there at all. Like the waves out at sea, one day she would feel furious and powerful, as though she could sweep aside anything that got in her way; another day she would be calm, becalmed even, tranquil, still and at peace. One day she would be deep and mysterious, as though sunken treasure and strange realms lived below her calm and smooth surface; and the next she would be playful and light, like bubbles and foam whipped up by an afternoon breeze.

So Polly, who changed from one moment to the next, looked out at the world as it went about its business and wondered how she would ever fit in and find out who she really was.

One day, a young prince was riding down that busiest street in the busiest town in that particular sunny and dusty country, when he happened to look up at the window where Polly stood looking down, peeping out from behind her curtains.

"That girl is beautiful and wise and caring," he thought at once. "I would love to ask her if she will come with me to my palace and be my princess."

So he leapt off his horse and ran up the stairs to Polly's room, two at a time, and did just that. And Polly thought perhaps that was who she was, a princess. She was happy to have found out at last who she really was, so she agreed eagerly to go away with the prince and to be a princess and to live in his palace.

For some months Polly lived in a grand palace with the prince as his princess. She wore a different beautiful dress every day, made of coloured silk and rare feathers and crushed flowers and fabrics embroidered with gold. She went to endless banquets where she was always the most beautiful woman in the room, and she stayed by the side of her prince, except when he had to discuss matters of state with his father the king, or when he was touring the land meeting the people. For in that particular sunny, dusty country that was not what princesses did at all.

But one day the prince, who was very kind and really loved Polly very much, said to her, "Polly, my princess, I can see that you are not truly happy here. When I looked up at that window a year ago, I saw behind those curtains someone who was beautiful and wise and caring. But here, although you are more beautiful than any other woman, I know you feel that you cannot truly be wise. For princesses here are allowed only to be beautiful and must not get involved with matters of state or visiting the people in the land. I cannot keep you any longer in this palace, which will become like a prison, you who are beautiful, wise and caring and who change like the moon and the sea. I cannot keep you here as my princess."

Sad as she was, Polly knew that the prince was right, so she agreed to leave. On the day she was to depart, as she walked for the last time down the long, candlelit corridors hung with purple silks, the king's chief advisor came hurrying towards her in somewhat of a fluster.

"Ah, Polly," he said, his face red and his moustache twirling up at the edges, "I wonder if you can perhaps help me. You see, there are terrible and complex problems with some of the eastern countries neighbouring our fine kingdom. There are many treaties to be signed and negotiations to be made and, alas, perhaps even wars to be fought. You are so beautiful, wise and caring. Now you are no longer our princess, I wonder if you would, perhaps, maybe, consider being our ambassador in the Eastern Kingdom?"

And Polly thought perhaps that was who she was, not a princess at all, but an ambassador. She was happy to have found out at last who she must be, so she agreed to travel to the far corners of the Eastern Kingdom as the court ambassador, to try to negotiate with distant countries and strange noblemen.

For some months Polly did just this and met many foreign kings and princes and advisors and politicians and had many, many discussions. Her judgement was always wise. She would weigh up every angle and every possibility and her view was sharp and sound and many was the time she saved a desperate situation from turning into war. But with each treaty she negotiated and signed, she knew with a heavy heart that there were always those who lost out, who could not get what they wanted because they had no army, or no advisors, or no diplomats. And because she was wise she made many fine treaties, but also because she was wise she knew that many people would suffer, whatever treaty was signed.

And one day the chief advisor came to visit Polly in her house on the edge of the Eastern Kingdom on a matter of high importance, his face even redder and his moustache twirling even more sharply. But when he saw her, he shook his head sadly.

"Polly, my best ambassador, I see that you are not truly happy here. When I saw you in the corridor with the swirling, purple silks and the candles burning that day, I saw a woman who was beautiful and wise and caring. But although you are wiser than any in the Eastern Kingdom, I know you feel that you cannot truly be caring. For ambassadors must only be wise, and cannot spend their time caring for each single person who suffers when they sign a treaty, otherwise they will be forever sad. I cannot keep you here, you who are beautiful, wise and caring and who change like the moon and the sea. I cannot keep you here as my ambassador."

Polly was very sad to once again not know who she was. But she knew the chief advisor was right, so a few days later she packed her bags and left her house. She did not know where she was going or what would become of her. Once again, with a heavy heart, Polly wondered exactly how a girl who is always changing can find out who she really is.

She walked slowly away from her house and into the desert, with the sun burning down and the sand swirling around her in the wind. When she had been walking for a while, she saw a woman wearing just rags leading a skinny donkey on a piece of rope. The woman came up to Polly and smiled.

"Polly," she said, "perhaps you can help me. I know that you are truly beautiful and caring and wise. The people of my village some miles from here have suffered greatly with all the treaties and wars and different kings and armies that have passed through. There are many old people who are sick, and many young people who have lost their families and need to be taught. I wonder if you could come with me to our village to nurse the sick and teach the young."

And Polly thought perhaps that was who she was, not a princess or an ambassador, but a nurse and a teacher. She was happy to have found out finally who she really was, so she agreed to go with the lady and her donkey to the village.

For many months she worked every hour she could, caring for the old who were sick and for the young who had lost their parents and needed to be taught. As a nurse and a teacher there was no one finer. She healed many people and made them smile again. Many children grew strong and healthy and became clever and grew to love this foreign woman just as they had their own families.

But one day the woman with the donkey came towards Polly and smiled sadly.

"Polly, my kind and caring nurse and friend, I see that you are not happy here. When I saw you in the desert with the swirling sand and the sun burning that day, I saw someone who was beautiful and wise and caring. But here, although you are more caring than we could possibly have asked for and spend all your time helping and looking after others, I see that you do not feel beautiful. For a nurse in our village quickly becomes tired and worn out through caring all the time for others and cannot spend any time caring for themselves. I cannot keep you here, you who are beautiful, wise and caring and who change like the moon and the sea. I cannot keep you here as our dear nurse and teacher."

Polly was heartbroken to be leaving the children and the old people and her friend. And she was sad once again that she kept changing and never knew who she was. But she knew that her friend was right. So a few days later, with a heavy heart once again, she left the village and wandered for many days and nights from village to village knowing neither where she was going nor why.

Eventually, after a long time wandering, she found herself back in the busiest street in the busiest town in that sunny and dusty country, outside the door that led up to her room. By the side of the door sat an old, ugly beggar woman on a bright, woven blanket that was well worn and had many holes. The blanket was wet, as though the woman was sitting in a puddle.

"Who are you?" the old lady growled, as Polly brushed passed her.

"I don't know," sighed Polly sadly, "I am not a princess, nor an ambassador, nor a nurse or a teacher. Though people have said I am beautiful and wise and caring, I seem always to change from one minute to the next and so I cannot say who I am."

The old woman seemed to laugh to herself.

"Well my dear," she said, "if you truly want to find out who it is you are, I know of a place far away where you will find your answer. One week's ride to the north is the great northern forest. Inside the forest, by the side of a lake, is a tall tower with a copper roof. There at the very top is a room with a big oak door that has no handle. If you can find a way to open that door you will find your answer. And good luck to you," she laughed merrily, "you who are beautiful and wise and caring and who change from one minute to the next."

Well, Polly felt like she had nothing to lose. She had been to the prince's palace and to the far eastern corner of the kingdom and to a remote and simple village and still she seemed to change from one minute to the next. Still she did not know who she really was. So she packed her bag and began to walk towards the great northern forest.

For many, many days she walked alone, sleeping by the side of the road at night or occasionally coming across a barn or a shed to rest in. Sometimes she would meet people and travel with them for a while and they would share their food with her. When they asked her who she was, she had to admit she wasn't all that sure, and when they asked her where she was going, she also had to admit that she didn't really know. When they asked her why she was going there, she admitted yet again that she wasn't certain, and when they asked her who had told her to go there, she would tell them about a strange woman she had seen just once, sitting in a puddle. And she would wonder if she was mad.

After many days, Polly did finally arrive at the great northern forest. She entered the forest and walked for a few more days until eventually she saw a huge lake. The lake was completely surrounded by trees and at the farthest end Polly could indeed see a single tall tower with a green copper roof. She began to walk around the edge of the lake towards the tower, her pace quickening as she wondered if maybe, finally, she really would find out who she was. The lake was vast and it took all day for Polly to walk around its pebbled shore. But eventually, as night was falling, she found herself at the foot of the tower in front of an oak door.

This particular door had a large handle, and without thinking to knock, Polly pushed it breathlessly. The door swung open, smoothly and silently, which was rather odd since it looked like no one had opened it or even been near the tower for many years. Polly peered in. The tower was very, very tall and very, very narrow and the doorway she was now standing in led directly to a stone, spiral staircase that went straight up.

Polly wondered if she should wait until morning. After all, she was tired and from the look of the tower there would be an awful lot of stairs to climb. But although she was tired, she was also excited and her heart was beating quickly now. And because the moon was full tonight and was reflected by the lake, she felt that there was enough light for her to make her way.

So she began to climb. Up, up, round and round. Once in a while there was a small window cut into the side of the tower, which allowed a slender fragment of moonlight to come in and light the way. But that was all there seemed to be; no rooms, no people, just heavy stone stairs, round, round, up and up for what seemed like ages.

Polly was becoming very tired now. She began to wonder if it had been such a good idea to begin her climb tonight after all. There was absolutely no place to rest. Her only option seemed to be to keep climbing, no matter how exhausted she was becoming. On and on the stairs went, with just occasional moonlight to give the echoes of her steps on the stone stairs some company. Finally, after hours of climbing up, Polly saw that the stairs ended a few feet in front of her and were replaced by an oak door. It had no handle.

"This must be it," she whispered to herself. "This must be the door I have to open if I want to find out who I am."

She examined the door. There didn't seem to be any hidden handles. She gave it a small push. Nothing happened. She gave it a huge shove with whatever strength she had left. Maybe, just maybe the door seemed to move a fraction. She couldn't be sure.

There seemed to be nothing for it. After inspecting the door and feeling all over it and around the frame, Polly decided on the direct approach. She really was exhausted now, and had no idea what she would do if she couldn't open the door. She would just have to rest as best she could and make her long, long way down once it was light.

Polly walked down a few steps and paused. Then, summoning up all the energy and strength she had left, she ran up the steps and bounded straight towards the door, leaping with her whole body, shoulder first, to give it one big, final shove.

A funny thing happened then. As Polly flew through the air, straight for the door, it suddenly, silently, swung wide open, just like that. And Polly found herself flying straight into the room.

Except it wasn't a room at all and never had been.

In a brief moment of horror, she suddenly realised that the door had actually been on the outside of the tower and there was nothing behind it at all, except the night sky and a long, long drop. The old woman in the puddle had tricked her. Polly looked down and saw far, far below her the lake surrounded for miles around by the forest, a deep and silvery green in the light of the full moon. She desperately tried to grab hold of something, but it was too late. There was absolutely nothing to hold onto and she was falling, falling in the night sky, hurtling towards the lake below her.

The moon was full and was reflected perfectly in that vast, still lake, surrounded by the dark and silvery trees. It all looked so beautiful and her heart felt like it would burst, and she laughed, because she was surely about to die. It struck her as quite funny that she was laughing and this made her laugh some more. And then suddenly she started to cry, and her tears fell towards the lake. But because Polly was falling too, her tears just accompanied her on her way down, tiny little droplets of water falling with her and around her, through the clear night-time sky. And each single teardrop reflected the round face of the moon.

As she fell, it was as though she was falling into the moon itself. As she hurtled towards the lake, the moon became larger and larger and Polly could see not just the moon but thousands of stars also reflected in the vast, still lake. And in each of the tears that danced and spun around her, she could see another moon and a thousand more stars. And as she fell, Polly was twisting and turning through the silent night sky, so all at once she could no longer tell if she was falling down or up. When she looked up, there was the bright circle of the moon surrounded by stars; and when she looked down, there was another moon surrounded by exactly the same stars.

Suddenly Polly had no idea at all what was down and what was up. All she knew was that she was speeding and spinning towards the moon and that it was becoming bigger and bigger and brighter and brighter.

would she get wet or would she bang her head on the crusty surface of the moon? Would it be made of cheese? She laughed again at the strange thoughts of one about to die. And the sound of her laughter echoed back from the trees as she fell.

And then she realised with a shock that she wasn't moving at all. She was just floating, suspended with a huge, round moon all around her and just when she was wondering what that could possibly mean …

Plop! Splash! Polly had dived through the surface of the moon, piercing its silver skin. Her tears had accompanied her all the way along this miraculous journey and now each one became a moon surrounding her and lighting her way as she fell towards the centre. Down and down she seemed to go and gradually the lights began to fade and after some time all was still, silent and black.

And then, in an instant, once more there was light.

Polly opened her eyes. It was daytime and she was sitting in a busy street in a particular sunny, dusty country that she recognised at once as her home. By her side was the old beggar woman who looked at her and chuckled softly. Had it all just been a dream or a curse or a spell?

"Well deary, looks like we'd better get you out of those clothes," said the old woman.

Polly looked down. Although the sun was high in the sky and all was dusty around her, her clothes were wet as though she had been sitting in a puddle or a lake, or had dived to the centre of the moon.

"Let's get you changed, my dear," said the old woman kindly. And then she chuckled softly to herself, "That's assuming you don't mind changing, of course."

And Polly knew that she was always changing. She smiled and knew that of course she would never, could never stay the same from one moment to the next.

She looked up at all the people coming and going in the street.

There was a soldier marching off to battle. Though he marched boldly, Polly saw in his eyes that he was scared. Scared of what might happen, that he might lose his life or have to take another's.

And she saw a grocer selling his colourful fruit and vegetables. In his eyes she saw that though he shouted loudly about how cheap and fresh his wares were, he was worried about whether he would have enough to feed and clothe his family at the end of each day.

And Polly saw a woman with young children. Although she told them what to do and led them about, she saw in the woman's eyes that she was sad that they would one day leave her and that she had no idea what the world would have in store for any of them.

Polly who was beautiful and wise and caring felt tears welling up inside her once more, and she knew that everything and everyone is always changing from one moment to the next and would never be the same. And although she was sad, still she felt joy that anything was possible and everything was changing.

From that day onwards, Polly lived happily in her light, white room, behind clean cotton curtains on the busiest street in the busiest town in that particular sunny, dusty country. Every day she would come down from her room and walk around the street, smiling to the soldiers as they marched off to war, thanking the grocers for their wonderful fruit and laughing with the children who played in the street.

And everyone was so happy to have someone with them who was beautiful and caring and wise, in a world where no one and nothing is certain.

The Story of Oswald Bat

One day Oswald Bat was doing what he did every day. Hanging upside down, together with many hundreds of other bats, all curled up in the roof of their dark cave. There were bats just like Oswald Bat tucked into nooks and crannies everywhere and clinging onto stalactites that pointed to the rocky floor below. You see, as you may already know, bats only come out at night, when it is dark. During the day they stay in their caves hanging upside down, waiting until they can go out to hunt, waiting for the sun (which they have never, ever seen) to fade and for night to come. This is how it had been for thousands upon thousands upon thousands of years. This is what bats did. And there were few complaints.

But something troubled Oswald that day. Hanging in the darkness with all the other bats, his heart was full and swollen like a fruit ready to fall from a vine. You see, Oswald Bat had had dreams, thoughts, and notions of another life, a place of shapes and strangeness, breezes and warmth. Where these dreams came from he had no idea, but that they would not go away and that they became stronger and stronger every day was clear to him. Oswald Bat had told the other bats of these visions and of his strange desire one day to remain outside the cave when it was no longer dark.

"Don't be a fool, Oswald," they chided. "It has been this way for thousands upon thousands upon thousands of years. We bats stay in the darkness of our caves and go out at night. No bat who stays outside of the cave once the darkness fades can ever return – they will be blinded and burnt and lose their way. They will be confused and ruined and forget where they belong. They will become mad and sick and forget who they are."

But Oswald was still troubled by these dreams and feelings of a strange, wonderful place, though neither he nor any bat had seen it. And though the darkness was a friend, he felt sure in a way he could never describe that he was also its slave. Though darkness allowed him to leave his cave, he felt sure that it sought also to keep him there.

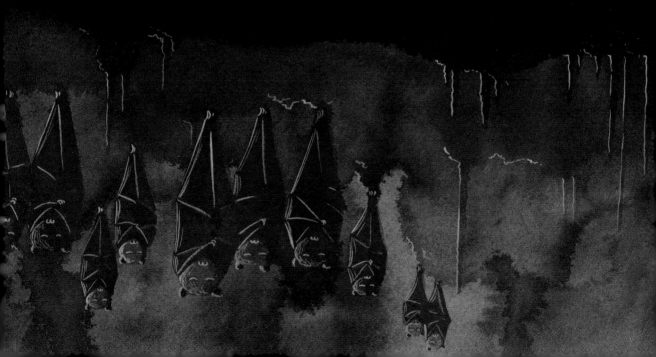

The only other bat who would listen when he spoke of all this was his friend, Sue Bat. Sue would listen for hours, enraptured by these stories of far off places, though she too had no idea of what they could mean or where such a place could possibly be.

Every night, once the darkness reigned outside and had entered fully into the cave, the bats would leave as they had for thousands upon thousands upon thousands of years and go flying and hunting. And well before the darkness began to fade, they would return to the safety and certainty of their cave.

But on that particular evening, when he flew out of the cave, Oswald decided that he wouldn't come back with the other bats. Despite all he had been told about the land outside of darkness, he was determined to find out for himself what it was like. Though he was terrified of being blinded and ruined and mad, that night he stayed out just a few minutes later than the others.

With all the other bats safely back inside, Oswald sat quietly on the branch of a bouble tree at the edge of the forest. As the shrill shrieking of the bats died down, he heard another sound in the trees and, for the first time ever in his life, something strange entered the darkness of his eyes.

It was too much. He felt like he must be blind and mad. The noise so close to him was unlike anything he had ever heard, and the tiny flicker of something that wasn't darkness hurt his eyes and made him dizzy and confused. Maybe it was true what the other bats had said after all.

So Oswald flew straight back to the cave. The other bats had not yet noticed his absence, apart from Sue. She said nothing, but waited silently beside him, listening as his quick, frantic breathing slowly returned to normal.

A few days later, Oswald decided that he would try again. As the other bats returned to the cave, with the darkness still a blanket around them, he stayed once more on the branch of a bouble tree on the edge of the forest for just a few extra moments. Again he heard a noise, though this time it didn't scare or disturb him – he found it strange and curious but not altogether unpleasant. And, as before, a vivid flicker of non-darkness swam through his mind – but it was less painful this time, and interesting, and Oswald's heart beat faster as the flicker danced through him. So Oswald stayed out a little longer. Then more sounds came and they were all around him. Different sensations seemed suddenly to attack him as the non-darkness in his eyes became a fevered and swirling medley, that again made him dizzy and sick and fear that he would go mad.

So once again he headed quickly back to his cave and hung in the dark, breathing fast, trembling slightly, as his friend Sue listened and said nothing.

For many weeks and months Oswald Bat would leave the cave with the other bats but return a little later and then a little later still, waiting a while on the branch of a bouble tree at the edge of the forest. He began to like the different patterns of non-darkness, the flickering lights and shades and the strange sounds, the echoes and whistles that happened just at the edge of night. He would come back to the cave later and later and hang upside down next to his friend, Sue Bat. And mostly his breathing

Finally, early one morning, with the other bats all returned to their cave, Oswald Bat was sitting on the branch of a bouble tree at the edge of the forest as the darkness around him evaporated. The many wonderful patterns of non-darkness began to flicker and flutter around him.

"Go back," a voice in his head urged. "For no one can return who has seen the daylight." Oswald was gripped with fear when he heard this word. He knew that this thing, whatever it was, this strange, fearsome thing that some called the sun, was about to rise. He knew for sure that any bat who saw it would go blind and become mad and forget who he was.

"Go back now," the voice urged, "while you still can."

Trembling, Oswald began to fly. Whether he was already mad or not, who knows, but he found he was flying with all his strength, not towards the cave, but in the opposite direction towards where the colours flickered brightest and most vivid. Towards where a breathtaking and wonderful ball of extreme non-darkness began to rise up somewhere in front of him.

For the first time in all his life Oswald Bat flew towards the sun.

It was blinding. And the noises around him were deafening. The winds and heat and leaves that brushed against him felt scorching and overwhelming and raw. The patterns of non-darkness all around danced and leapt and swirled in a thousand ways all at once. And the noises echoed and bounced and sang and wavered endlessly, while the breezes seemed to catch him and lift him higher and higher towards the sun. Oswald flew like he had never flown before.

He could feel the breezes speed him onwards towards the dancing colours of non-darkness and suddenly he could see, really see, colours, shades, reflections and movement all around him. The forest in which he had flown all his life suddenly appeared to him.

The calling of its many creatures suddenly became clear, surrounding him for miles and miles. As the breeze lifted him, he looked and saw that his wings were feathered and large, where he had always thought them smooth and black. He saw that he was magnificent, fast and swooping where he had always felt himself small and flapping. Oswald rose higher and higher and his vision was forever where before he had seen nothing. Now he was no longer blind, he was no longer mad. Now he had remembered who he was. The sun rose fully for the first time and greeted Oswald warmly as he soared miles above the forest, seeing, feeling, hearing everything around him. And miles below, in a single raindrop falling from a single drooping leaf on the branch of a bouble tree, he saw reflected the whole world.

That day Sue Bat was hanging in her cave and as time passed Oswald did not return as she was used to. All day she waited but still he did not return.

The other bats noticed this. "The fool," they said, "he didn't listen to us and now he is surely blind and mad and he has forgotten where he belongs and who he is. Let that be a lesson to us," they said, nodding their heads, "those of us with mad ideas."

Indeed it was a lesson to all the bats. For the very next day they all went back to their cave especially early, way before the darkness could begin to creep away. Apart from one. A trembling Sue Bat stayed on the branch of a bouble tree for a few brief moments. The first flickers of non-darkness were painful and blinding and the first breath of warmth felt like it would burn. And as she headed back to the safety of her cave she heard a strange, strange sound.

Only many, many months later, as she too soared towards the sun, did she discover that it was the sound of an eagle, with wings of gold and freedom, and eyes that could see beyond the stars.

The Rainbow Bridge of the Sea

Once there was a sailor and he sailed the seas day after day, year after year without ever (or almost ever) going to land. He loved the sea and all its creatures; its sights and sounds; the vast, crimson sunsets and the tear-filled, innocent sunrises. He loved the endless surprises of the sea; the storms, the winds, the baking hot stillness on the Indian Ocean at the height of summer, with the sun a blazing ball of orange for days without end. He loved the many visitors to his ship; the huge-winged seabirds in the howling winter, and the busy, chattering flocks of bright yellow canaries and tiny, emerald parakeets whenever he sailed near to tropical islands. He loved the dolphins who leapt out of the cool, azure water and played around his ship for hours with no thought of better things to do. And he was awed by the huge creatures of the sea, the mysterious whales rising like islands and calling across the ocean, in the deepest blues and darkest purples of the night.

But much as he loved the sea and all that was in it, the sailor was looking for something. It was this one thing that had led him to the sea all those years ago and which kept him sailing endlessly across the oceans, forever in hope. The sailor, like many before him, was searching for the rainbow bridge of the sea.

Many had heard of the rainbow bridge, some claimed they had seen it from afar. No one knows how many had actually found it. For it was said that somewhere in the sea was a rainbow bridge, and that whoever found it would be transported to whatever sort of place they wished for. Some said the bridge led to paradise, others to whatever the heart desired. Villagers and townspeople believed it led to hidden, far off lands under the sea. For pirates and adventurers it was the gateway to a magical world, where the trees shone with diamonds and the wind blew through trees with golden leaves.

No one was really sure, however, because although many had thought they had seen the rainbow bridge of the sea, once they sailed towards it, they found again and again that it was just a normal rainbow, which disappeared as fast as they approached it.

It was this that the sailor had been seeking his whole life as he sailed across the seas. At night he would dream about the special place he hoped to discover when finally he found the rainbow bridge. He would lie awake when the sea was rough or the weather still and hot, imagining it in all its detail. But though he had seen hundreds of rainbows and chased each of them, so far every one had evaporated without trace, disappearing mirage-like back into the sea.

When on occasion he put into land and visited markets or the occasional inn, the sailor would hear more stories from folk who claimed to have seen the rainbow bridge of the sea or to know where it was.

Slowly, over many years of searching, the sailor became rich, taking goods from one part of the world to the other, ferrying wealthy passengers over the sea. He bought a bigger ship, beautifully decorated and elegantly furnished. In a village of many coloured sand, overlooking the Indian Ocean, the sailor met a woman and they fell in love. In time they were married and had three children, and then they all sailed together across the sea. And still the sailor searched for the rainbow bridge.

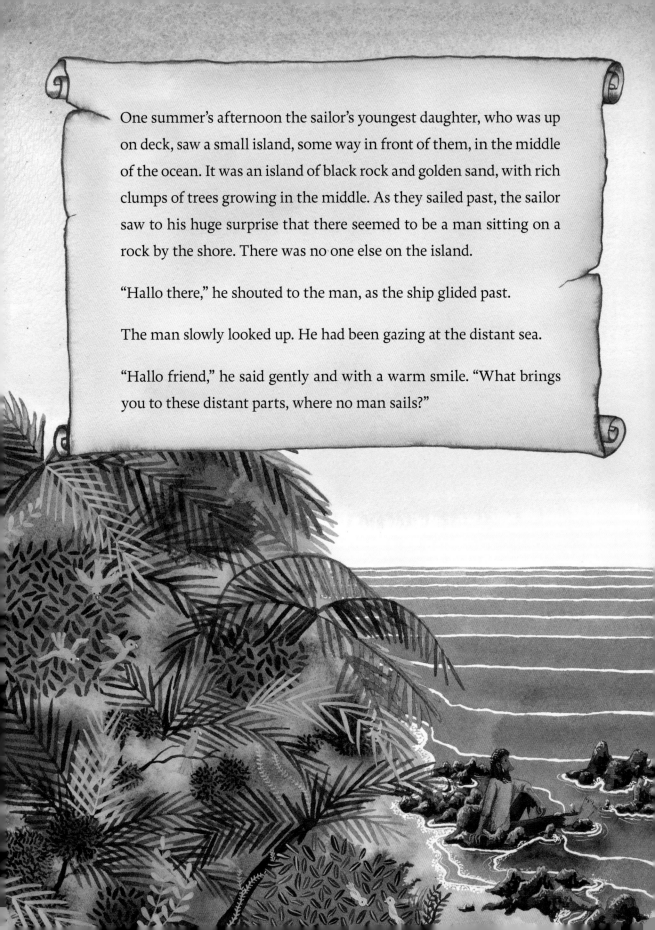

One summer's afternoon the sailor's youngest daughter, who was up on deck, saw a small island, some way in front of them, in the middle of the ocean. It was an island of black rock and golden sand, with rich clumps of trees growing in the middle. As they sailed past, the sailor saw to his huge surprise that there seemed to be a man sitting on a rock by the shore. There was no one else on the island.

"Hallo there," he shouted to the man, as the ship glided past.

The man slowly looked up. He had been gazing at the distant sea.

"Hallo friend," he said gently and with a warm smile. "What brings you to these distant parts, where no man sails?"

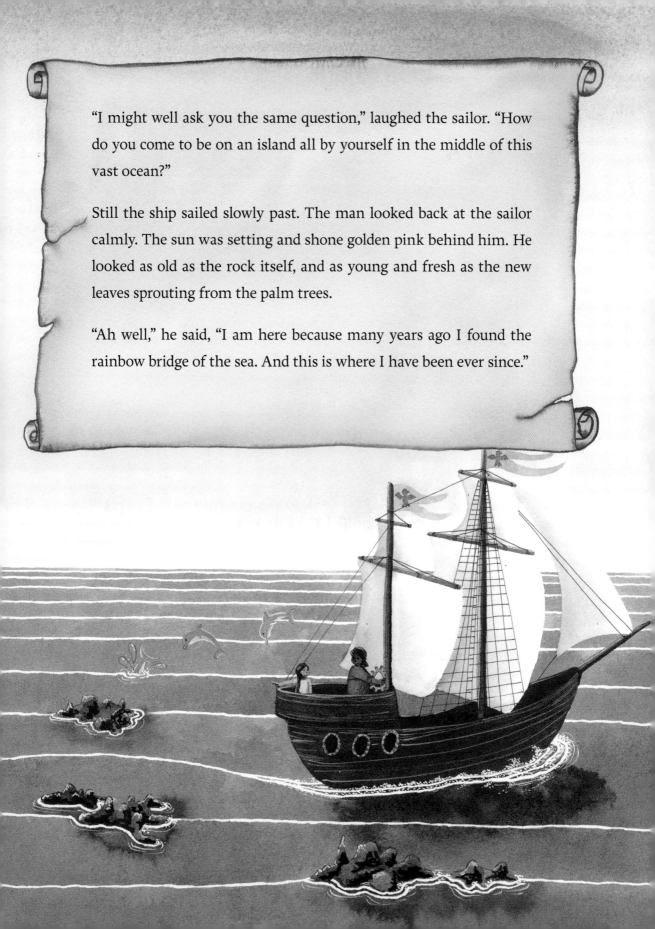

"I might well ask you the same question," laughed the sailor. "How do you come to be on an island all by yourself in the middle of this vast ocean?"

Still the ship sailed slowly past. The man looked back at the sailor calmly. The sun was setting and shone golden pink behind him. He looked as old as the rock itself, and as young and fresh as the new leaves sprouting from the palm trees.

"Ah well," he said, "I am here because many years ago I found the rainbow bridge of the sea. And this is where I have been ever since."

The sailor was stunned. He could barely talk. His spine tingled and a wave of warmth shivered through his body.

"You have found the rainbow bridge of the sea?" he gasped.

"I have," replied the man.

"And are you happy here, all by yourself on this island?" asked the sailor.

"Sometimes I am happy, and sometimes I am not, but always here is where I wish to be."

"Can you tell me where I can find the rainbow bridge?" shouted the sailor. The ship was nearly beyond the island now, the water too deep to lay anchor.

"I cannot tell you where to find it. But I can tell you this. Everyone who looks for the rainbow bridge of the sea thinks only about where they want to go when they finally find it. But to find the rainbow bridge you must truly know where it is you start from. Then perhaps you will find it."

The last words died off in the distance as the ship sailed past the island.

"Farewell, friend," thought the sailor to himself. "May your days on your island be good."

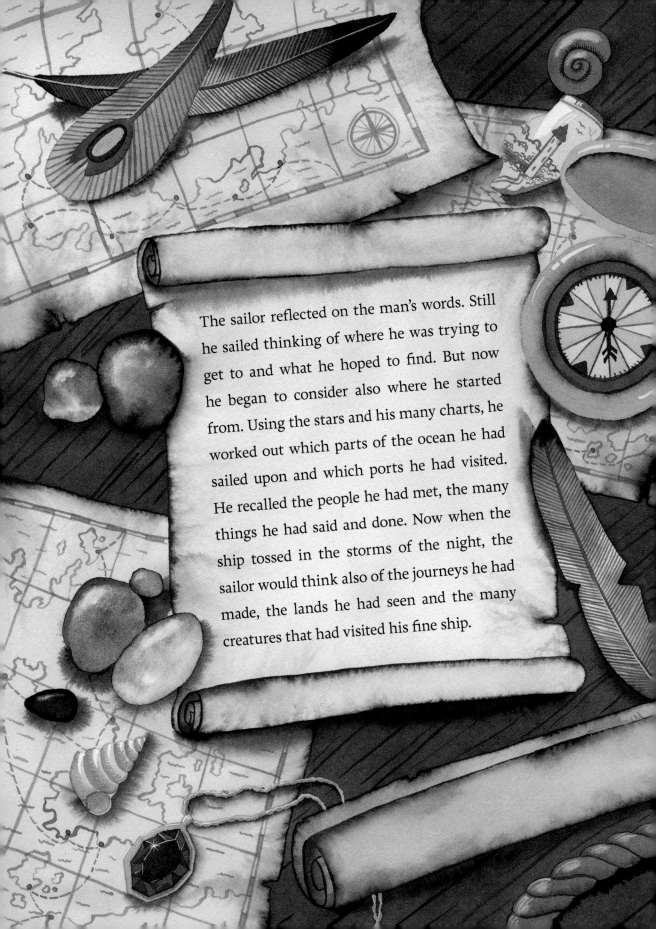

The sailor reflected on the man's words. Still he sailed thinking of where he was trying to get to and what he hoped to find. But now he began to consider also where he started from. Using the stars and his many charts, he worked out which parts of the ocean he had sailed upon and which ports he had visited. He recalled the people he had met, the many things he had said and done. Now when the ship tossed in the storms of the night, the sailor would think also of the journeys he had made, the lands he had seen and the many creatures that had visited his fine ship.

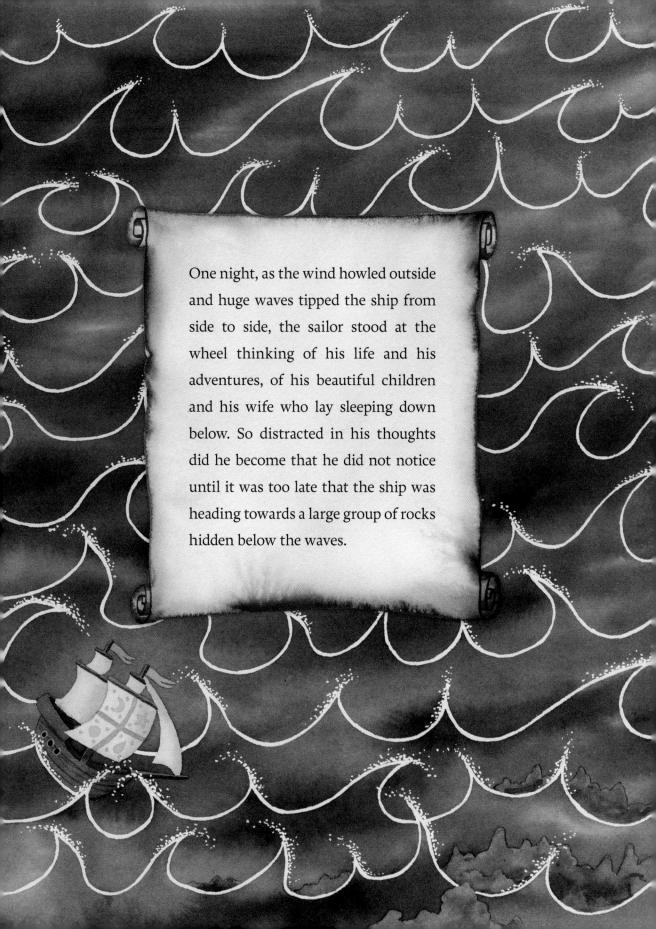

One night, as the wind howled outside and huge waves tipped the ship from side to side, the sailor stood at the wheel thinking of his life and his adventures, of his beautiful children and his wife who lay sleeping down below. So distracted in his thoughts did he become that he did not notice until it was too late that the ship was heading towards a large group of rocks hidden below the waves.

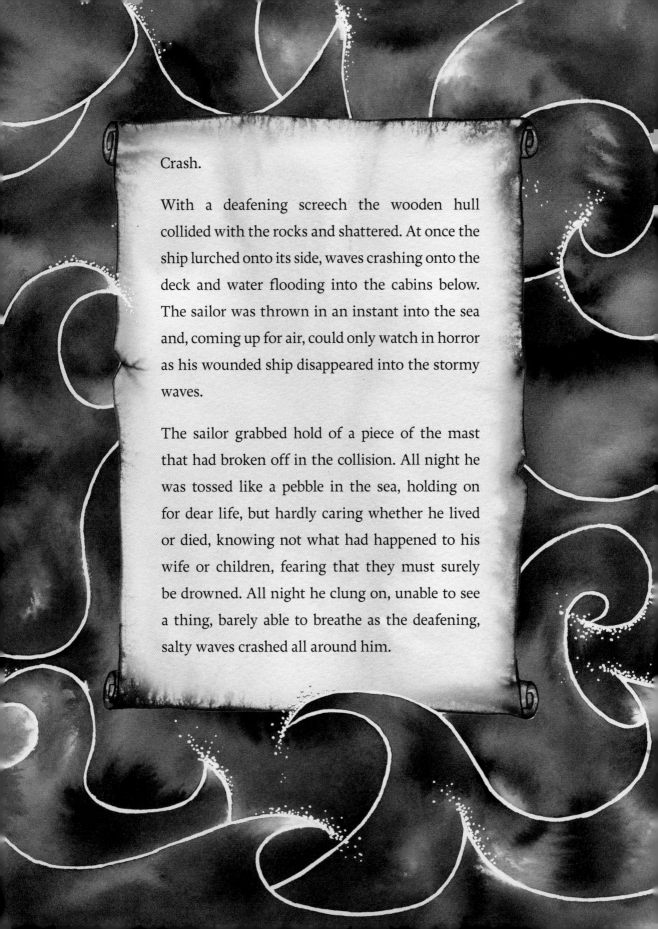

Crash.

With a deafening screech the wooden hull collided with the rocks and shattered. At once the ship lurched onto its side, waves crashing onto the deck and water flooding into the cabins below. The sailor was thrown in an instant into the sea and, coming up for air, could only watch in horror as his wounded ship disappeared into the stormy waves.

The sailor grabbed hold of a piece of the mast that had broken off in the collision. All night he was tossed like a pebble in the sea, holding on for dear life, but hardly caring whether he lived or died, knowing not what had happened to his wife or children, fearing that they must surely be drowned. All night he clung on, unable to see a thing, barely able to breathe as the deafening, salty waves crashed all around him.

Many hours later, as dawn broke, the waters began to calm and the sun began to rise. The sailor looked around him. He saw nothing. There was no sign of his ship, or his wife or children, and no land in sight. He realised he was hungry and thirsty. The sun rose higher in the sky and burned down on him. He had used all his strength to survive the night's storm and now he realised he had barely any left and was at the mercy of the wind and the waves.

"I have lost everything," thought the sailor to himself, as he weakly held on to the broken mast. "I have lost my ship, with all its fine decorations and furnishings. I have lost those I love, with little hope of finding them again. I have lost everything I own, my riches and my treasures, my charts and maps. I am totally alone with nothing at all. I am at the mercy of the sea and the waves. Any minute I will surely lose my life."

The sea was perfectly calm and still now, like a mirror of polished crystal reflecting the vast ocean sky. As the sun rose, the sailor saw a beautiful rainbow appear in the distance. It was odd to see a rainbow suddenly appear in a clear, dawn sky, with neither rain nor mist.

Still not caring whether he lived or died, the sailor allowed the tide to carry him towards the rainbow, and as he came closer and closer he found that it did not disappear, but began to shine more vividly, its colours clear and jewel-like.

Then he realised that through the mercy of the wind and the waves and the sea he had finally found the rainbow bridge of the sea.

The sailor smiled and let go of the piece of mast he was holding on to.

And what happened to him then, where he found himself and who was waiting for him when he arrived may be known but cannot be said.

Acknowledgements

First and foremost, we owe huge thanks to Sarah Bird for her enthusiasm, encouragement, generosity and most of all patience, in helping us bring these stories to life.

Thank you to Alan Blakemore, Amelia Jenkins and Nicole Wootton-Cane for their invaluable help in copy-editing and proof-reading, and to Melanie Newman and Alison Kennedy for sage and generous advice throughout.

Big thanks as well to Bill Norris at Central Books and Jim Sheehan at Signature, and our patient printers, CPI Books.

We are extremely grateful to Tom Passmore and Nathan Baranowski for their help in facilitating our crowd-funding project.

Thank you to Chris Seeley for hosting Tim's writing retreat at the lovely Folly Cottage.

This book's creation has also been supported by a lovely team of 'godparents': a big thank you to Rupesh Shah, Pete Sutton, Rosie Godfrey and Luke Foster.

We are so grateful to have had the energy and support of Iva Carrdus in so many different and wonderful ways, not least helping Katie get it all together at the eleventh hour. Thank you.

Finally, without the generous financial support from everyone who responded to our crowd-funding campaign this book may never have happened. To you we owe the greatest thanks of all.

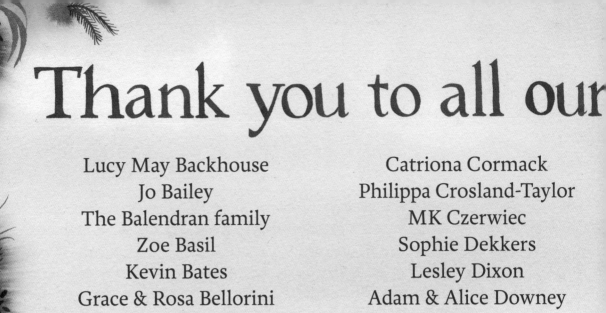

Thank you to all our

Lucy May Backhouse
Jo Bailey
The Balendran family
Zoe Basil
Kevin Bates
Grace & Rosa Bellorini
David Bent-Hazelwood
Dan Betterton
The Bingham family
Alex Bird
Tom & Louisa Borrett
Tilly Boscott
Chantal Bourgonje
Linda Broadbent
Steve Bullock
Lily & Meg Byrne
Mary Cade
Graham Calvert
Mary Campbell
Penny Campbell
Elvey Carrdus
Rodica Cioplea
Anna Connor

Catriona Cormack
Philippa Crosland-Taylor
MK Czerwiec
Sophie Dekkers
Lesley Dixon
Adam & Alice Downey
Molly & Myles Downey
Gill Dunn
Sophie Easteal
Elizabeth Edwards
Marvin Fernandes
Victoria Finlay
Marika Finne
Claire Fisher
Luke Foster
Alexandra Foster
Flora Galloway
Emily Gillingham
Rosie Godfrey
Sally Gray
Graham & Rosie Green
David Gullen
Edward Halsted
Kati & Maia Harris-Jordan

lovely supporters...

Ulrike Haug	Mira Preist
Steve Hinde	Anna-Elise Price
Johnathan Keen	Philip Raby
Aijung Kim	Micheline Rayner
Janee Lookerse	Yvonne Redgrave
Gary Luff	Nic Rigby
Mita Mahato	John & Lou Robinson
Sally Malnick	Penny Russell
Itai Marks	Oliver & Nicole Sanders
Geoff Mead	Rupesh & Kaajal Shah
Bonnie Millard	Rami Shah
Eddie & Lucy Millington	Michael Shannon
Jasmine Morris	Lochan Shand
Philippa Munro	Helen Stephens
Josephine Nelson	Lottie & Millie Stringer
Charlotte, Matilda	Pete Sutton
& William Nelson	Mark Terry
Ben Nicholson	Bryony Thiele
Neil O'Doherty	Barbara Turner-Vesselago
Chris Packe	Vicki Whittaker
Shabira Papain	Elizabeth Wilson
Kate Parsons	Peter Wise
Marian Partington	Paul Young
Rob Porteous	

www.thecrystalmirror.co.uk